FRANK WOOD'S
BUSINESS ACCOUNTING

MULTIPLE-CHOICE QUESTION BOOK

Tommy Robinson

LONDON • HONG KONG • JOHANNESBURG
MELBOURNE • SINGAPORE • WASHINGTON DC

FINANCIAL TIMES MANAGEMENT
128 Long Acre, London WC2E 9AN
Tel: +44 (0)171 447 2000
Fax: +44 (0)171 240 5771

A Division of Financial Times Professional Limited

**Visit the Financial Times Management website at
www.ftmanagement.com**

First published in Great Britain in 1998

© Financial Times Professional Limited 1998

The right of Tommy Robinson to be identified as author
of this work has been asserted by him in accordance with
the Copyright, Designs and Patents Act 1988.

ISBN 0 273 62545 4

British Library Cataloguing in Publication Data
A CIP catalogue record for this book can be obtained from the British Library

All rights reserved; no part of this publication may be reproduced, stored
in a retrieval system, or transmitted in any form or by any means, electronic,
mechanical, photocopying, recording, or otherwise without either the prior
written permission of the Publishers or a licence permitting restricted copying
in the United Kingdom issued by the Copyright Licensing Agency Ltd,
90 Tottenham Court Road, London W1P 9HE. This book may not be lent,
resold, hired out or otherwise disposed of by way of trade in any form of
binding or cover other than that in which it is published, without the prior
consent of the Publishers.

10 9 8 7 6 5 4 3 2 1

Printed and bound in Great Britain

The Publishers' policy is to use paper manufactured from sustainable forests.

Contents

Section	Title	Questions	Answers
1	The Accounting Equation and the Balance Sheet	1	101
2	The Double-Entry System for Assets, Liabilities and Capital	3	103
3	The Asset of Stock	4	104
4	The Effect of Profit or Loss on Capital and the Double-Entry System for Expenses and Revenues	6	105
5	Balancing Off Accounts	7	106
6	The Trial Balance	8	107
7	Trading and Profit and Loss Accounts: An Introduction	10	108
8	Balance Sheets	11	109
9	Trading and Profit and Loss Accounts and Balance Sheets: Further Considerations	14	111
10	Accounting Concepts	17	112
11	Books of Original Entry and Ledgers	19	114
12	The Banking System	20	114
13	Cash Books	22	115
14	The Sales Journal and the Sales Ledger	23	116
15	The Purchases Journal and the Purchases Ledger	24	116
16	The Returns Journals	25	116
17	The Journal	26	117
18	The Analytical Petty Cash Book and the Imprest System	26	117
19	Value Added Tax	27	117
20	Columnar Day Books	31	120
21	Employees' Pay	32	120
22	Computers and Accounting	33	120
23	Depreciation of Fixed Assets: Nature and Calculations	34	121
24	Double-Entry Records for Depreciation	38	124
25	Capital and Revenue Expenditure	41	126
26	Bad Debts, Provisions for Bad Debts, Provisions for Discounts on Debtors	42	126
27	Other Adjustments for Final Accounts	44	127
28	The Valuation of Stock	48	129
29	Bank Reconciliation Statements	51	131
30	Control Accounts	54	133
31	Errors not Affecting Trial Balance Agreement	61	135
32	Suspense Accounts and Errors	62	136
33	Introduction to Accounting Ratios	63	137
34	Single Entry and Incomplete Records	65	138
35	Receipts & Payments Accounts and Income & Expenditure Accounts	67	139
36	Manufacturing Accounts	69	140
37	Departmental Accounts	73	141
38	Partnership Accounts: An Introduction	74	142
39	Goodwill in Partnership Accounts	76	143
40	Partnership Accounts Continued: The Revaluation of Assets	77	143
41	An Introduction to the Final Accounts of Limited Liability Companies	78	143
42	Purchase of Existing Partnership and Sole Traders' Businesses	86	147
43	Cash Flow Statements: An Introduction	86	148
44	An Introduction to the Analysis and Interpretation of Accounting Statements	91	150
45	Accounting Theory	99	154
	Answers and Explanations	100	
	Answers - Quick Reference Table	155	

Preface

This book has been written in order to satisfy two needs.

The first is the need for a bank of self-test questions for use by students while they are learning accounting.

The second is the need for exam-style revision material for students sitting examination papers which include multiple-choice questions. Students will be pleased to know that many of the questions in this book are reproduced from such examinations.

Attempting the questions

There are four alternate solutions presented for each question in this book. Only one of these solutions is correct. You should study each question carefully until you have decided on the correct answer. When you have done this for the group of questions which you are attempting at any one time, you should look at the answers which are given on page 155.

If, for any question, your answer is not the same as that given, you should first reconsider your answer. If you cannot figure out why the indicated answer is correct, you should look at the explanations given on pages 100–154. If you are still unsure, you should re-read the relevant chapter in *Business Accounting 1* – the chapter number is referred to at the beginning of each section.

Note
Questions are not all meant to be equally time-consuming; it will take you much longer to do some questions than others.

Tommy Robinson

Section 1

The Accounting Equation and the Balance Sheet

If you have difficulty with any of the questions in this section, you should refer to Chapter 1 of **Frank Wood's Business Accounting 1** *(Seventh edition)*

1.1 Which of the following is an asset of a firm ?

    A   Machinery owned by the firm.

    B   Money owed by the firm to one of its suppliers in respect of goods purchased on credit.

    C   An overdrawn balance on the firm's bank account.

    D   The capital of the firm.

1.2 Which of the following is a liability of a firm ?

    A   A building owned by the firm.

    B   Cash in the firm's safe.

    C   Money owed to the firm by its debtors.

    D   Money which the firm has borrowed and has not yet repaid.

1.3 Which of the following equations is correct ?

A	Assets	+	Capital	=	Liabilities	
B	Liabilities	−	Capital	=	Assets	
C	Capital	=	Assets	+	Liabilities	
D	Capital	=	Assets	−	Liabilities	

1.4 Which of the following is correct ?

	Assets	*Liabilities*	*Capital*
A	£7,850	£1,250	£6,600
B	£8,200	£2,800	£11,000
C	£9,550	£1,150	£8,200
D	£5,420	£6,540	£1,120

1.5 The following is a list of the assets and liabilities of a firm at a particular date.

Premises owned by the firm	£ 20,000
Money owed by the firm to its creditors	3,000
Stock owned by the firm	8,500
Loan received by the firm from a bank	4,000
Cash in the firm's safe	100

The firm's capital at that date is:
- A £21,100
- B £21,600
- C £32,400
- D None of the above.

1.6 When a firm pays one of its creditors by cheque, the effect on its assets and liabilities is:

	Effect upon Assets	*Effect upon Liabilities*
A	Reduce bank	Reduce creditors
B	Increase bank	Increase creditors
C	Reduce bank	Increase creditors
D	None of the above	

1.7 When a firm lodges money which it received from one of its debtors, the effect on its assets and / or liabilities is:

	Effect upon Assets	*Effect upon Liabilities*
A	Reduce bank	Reduce creditors
B	Increase bank	Decrease debtors
C	Increase cash	Decrease loan
D	Increase stock	Decrease capital

1.8 The effect on a firm's assets and / or liabilities as a result of it being granted a bank loan and the amount of the loan being transferred into its bank current account is:

	Effect upon Assets	*Effect upon Liabilities*
A	Decrease bank	Decrease loan
B	Decrease bank	Increase loan
C	Increase bank	Increase loan
D	None of the above	

1.9 The effect on a firm's assets and / or liabilities as a result of it buying goods on credit is:

	Effect upon Assets	*Effect upon Liabilities*
A	Reduce bank	Reduce creditors
B	Increase cash	No effect
C	Increase cash	Decrease loan
D	Increase stock	Increase capital

Section 2

The Double-Entry System for Assets, Liabilities and Capital

If you have difficulty with any of the questions in this section, you should refer to Chapter 2 of **Frank Wood's Business Accounting 1** *(Seventh edition)*

2.1 Which of the following statements is correct ?

- A To record an increase in any given asset account that account must be debited.
- B To record a decrease in capital, the capital account must be credited.
- C To record an increase in any given liability account that account must be debited.
- D To record a decrease in any given liability account that account must be credited.

2.2 Which of the following possible double-entries is correct ?

	Account to Debit	*Account to Credit*
A	Bank	Bank
B	Vehicles	Bank
C	Both of the above.	
D	None of the above.	

2.3 A school bought a computer, which it intends to use for general administration, and paid for it by cheque. Which of the following double-entries is the correct way to record this transaction ?

	Account to Debit	*Account to Credit*
A	Computer	Bank
B	Bank	Computer
C	Cash	Computer
D	Computer	Cash

2.4 If there is a separate ledger account for each debtor and each creditor, which of the following double-entries is the correct way to record the lodgement of money received from P. Doyle, a debtor?

	Account to Debit	Account to Credit
A	P. Doyle	Bank
B	Bank	P. Doyle
C	Bank	Cash
D	Cash	P. Doyle

2.5 Which of the following double-entries is the correct way to record the lodgement of new capital into a firm's bank account?

	Account to Debit	Account to Credit
A	Capital	Bank
B	Cash	Capital
C	Bank	Capital
D	Capital	Cash

2.6 If there is a separate ledger account for each debtor and each creditor, which of the following double-entries is the correct way to record a cheque paid to B. Lee, a creditor?

	Account to Debit	Account to Credit
A	B. Lee	Cash
B	Bank	B. Lee
C	Cash	B. Lee
D	B. Lee	Bank

Section 3

The Asset of Stock

If you have difficulty with any of the questions in this section, you should refer to Chapter 3 of **Frank Wood's Business Accounting 1** *(Seventh edition)*

3.1 In accounting, the term 'purchases' means . . .

    A all items bought.

    B only goods bought on credit.

    C only those goods bought for resale.

    D only goods bought and paid for.

3.2 A newsagent's total sales includes the value of . . .

    A   any office furniture sold by him.

    B   office furniture sold by him, only if sold on credit.

    C   office furniture sold by him, only if sold for cash.

    D   None of the above.

3.3 Which of the following double-entries is the correct way to record the sale of goods, on credit, to R. Webb ?

	Account to Debit	Account to Credit
A	R. Webb	Sales
B	Returns inwards	R. Webb
C	Cash	Purchases
D	R. Webb	Returns inwards

3.4 In the accounts of K. Bryan, which of the following double-entries is the correct way to record goods returned by S. James, a credit customer ?

	Account to Debit	Account to Credit
A	Sales	K. Bryan
B	Returns inwards	S. James
C	Sales	S. James
D	S. James	Returns inwards

3.5 In the accounts of S. James, which of the following double-entries is the correct way to record goods returned by K. Bryan, a credit customer ?

	Account to Debit	Account to Credit
A	Sales	K. Bryan
B	Returns inwards	K. Bryan
C	Sales	S. James
D	S. James	Returns inwards

3.6 In the accounts of W. Balfe, which of the following double-entries is the correct way to record goods purchased from D. Connolly and paid for immediately in cash ?

	Account to Debit	Account to Credit
A	Sales	W. Balfe
B	Returns inwards	A O'Dea
C	Purchases	Cash
D	D. Connolly	Returns inwards

3.7 Which of the following double-entries is the correct way to record goods returned to A. Miller, a supplier?

	Account to Debit	Account to Credit
A	Sales	A. Miller
B	Returns inwards	A. Miller
C	Cash	Purchases
D	A. Miller	Returns outwards

Section 4

The Effect of Profit or Loss on Capital and the Double-Entry System for Expenses and Revenues

*If you have difficulty with any of the questions in this section, you should refer to Chapter 4 of **Frank Wood's Business Accounting 1** (Seventh edition).*

4.1 In the case of a sole trader . . .

- A earning profit does not affect capital.
- B earning profit reduces capital.
- C capital can arise only by earning profit.
- D earning profit increases capital.

4.2 In the case of a retail garage, which of the following double-entries is the correct way to record the lodgement of hire purchase commission received as a result of selling cars?

	Account to Debit	Account to Credit
A	Bank	Sales
B	Sales	Bank
C	Bank	Commission
D	None of the above.	

4.3 In the case of a DIY store, which of the following double-entries is the correct way to record the payment of rates for the current accounting period by cheque?

	Account to Debit	Account to Credit
A	Bank	Rates
B	Rates	Bank
C	Expenses	Bank
D	None of the above.	

4.4 In the case of a retail garage, which of the following double-entries is the correct way to record the payment, by cheque, of an electricity bill for the current accounting period ?

	Account to Debit	Account to Credit
A	Bank	Electricity
B	Electricity	Cash
C	Electricity	Bank
D	None of the above.	

Section 5

Balancing Off Accounts

If you have difficulty with any of the questions in this section, you should refer to Chapter 5 of **Frank Wood's Business Accounting 1** *(Seventh edition)*

5.1 What is the balance carried down on the following account on 31 May ?

P. Kelly

May 01	Sales	205	May 17	Bank	300
May 14	Sales	360	May 28	Returns Inwards	50
May 31	Sales	180			

- A £380 debit
- B £395 credit
- C £395 debit
- D None of the above.

5.2 What would the balance brought down on J. Barker's account be if it was balanced on June 19 ?

J. Barker

June 02	Sales	200	June 15	Bank	330
June 12	Sales	650	June 25	Returns Inwards	75
June 30	Sales	800			

- A £520 debit
- B £520 credit
- C £1,320 credit
- D None of the above.

5.3 Recording a single transaction in the double-entry accounting records may . . .

    A   increase the balance on an asset account by a given amount and decrease the balance on a liability account by the same amount.

    B   increase the balance on one asset account by a given amount and increase the balance on another asset account by the same amount.

    C   decrease the balance on a liability account by a given amount and decrease the balance on an asset account by the same amount.

    D   decrease the balance on an asset account by a given amount and increase the balance on a liability account by the same amount.

5.4 Which of the following transactions, on its own, could explain an increase in the debit balance brought down on the bank account in a firm's ledger ?

    A   The firm lodging money received from N. Taylor, a debtor.

    B   The purchase of stock by the firm.

    C   The firm repaying a bank loan.

    D   The firm paying money to one of its creditors.

Section 6
The Trial Balance

*If you have difficulty with any of the questions in this section, you should refer to Chapter 6 of **Frank Wood's Business Accounting 1** (Seventh edition)*

6.1 A firm's trial balance . . .

    A   shows its financial position.

    B   establishes whether its accounting records are correct.

    C   lists all of the entries in its double-entry accounting records.

    D   is a list of all of the balances brought down in its double-entry accounting records.

6.2 The purpose of a firm preparing a trial balance is to establish whether . . .

    A   the total of the debit balances brought down in its nominal (general) ledger equals that of the credit balances brought down.

    B   the double-entry record it has made for all transactions is correct.

    C   its bank balance is correct.

    D   it has earned a profit or incurred a loss.

6.3 The totals of a trial balance . . .

　　A　need not always agree, as there are sometimes legitimate reasons why they should differ.

　　B　should agree in all cases except when the trial balance is prepared at the end of an accounting period.

　　C　should always agree.

　　D　need not always agree, because the trial balance is not the same as a balance sheet.

6.4 An error of omission arises when . . .

　　A　either the debit entry or the credit entry for a particular transaction is recorded in the wrong class of ledger account.

　　B　a transaction is not entered at all in the nominal (general) ledger.

　　C　a correct figure is entered in the double-entry accounting records, but in the wrong person's account.

　　D　two errors are made, one of which cancels out the other.

6.5 An error of commission arises when . . .

　　A　either the debit entry or the credit entry for a particular transaction is recorded in the wrong class of ledger account.

　　B　a transaction is not recorded in the double-entry accounting records.

　　C　a correct figure is entered in the double-entry accounting records, once in the correct ledger account and once in the wrong person's account.

　　D　None of the above.

6.6 In the case of a newsagent's shop, which of the following is an error of principle ?

　　A　The cost of purchasing a photocopier on credit is entered on the debit side of the purchases account and on the credit side of the creditor's account.

　　B　A sale is not recorded in the double-entry accounting records.

　　C　A credit sale to A. Barker is entered on the credit side of the sales account and on the debit side of A. Baker's account.

　　D　None of the above.

6.7 An error of original entry occurs when . . .

　　A　either the debit entry or the credit entry for a particular transaction is recorded in the wrong class of account.

　　B　a correct figure is entered in the double-entry accounting records, once in the correct ledger account and once in the wrong person's account.

　　C　an incorrect figure is entered on the correct sides of the correct ledger accounts.

　　D　None of the above.

Section 7

Trading and Profit and Loss Accounts: An Introduction

If you have difficulty with any of the questions in this section, you should refer to Chapter 7 of **Frank Wood's Business Accounting 1** *(Seventh edition)*

7.1 Which of the following is prepared in order to determine a firm's net profit (or net loss) for an accounting period?

    A   A trading account.

    B   A profit and loss account.

    C   A trial balance.

    D   A balance sheet.

7.2 If the total of a firm's sales for the month of May is £300,000 and its gross profit is equal to 25% of its cost of sales, its cost of sales for May was:

    A   £60,000

    B   £75,000

    C   £225,000

    D   £240,000

7.3 The following information relates to a firm's trading during the month of June.

Gross profit for the month	£ 35,000
Expenses for the month	£ 18,000
Net profit for the month	equals 17% of the sales for the month

The firm's cost of sales for the month of June is:

    A   £52,000

    B   £53,000

    C   £65,000

    D   £100,000

7.4 If a sole trader's capital at the beginning of a year was £100,000 and his net profit for the year was £20,000, his capital at the end of the year . . .

    A   cannot be determined from the information given.

    B   was £80,000.

    C   was £100,000.

    D   was £120,000.

Section 8

Balance Sheets

If you have difficulty with any of the questions in this section, you should refer to Chapter 8 of **Frank Wood's Business Accounting 1** *(Seventh edition)*

8.1 A balance sheet is . . .

    A   a ledger account, proving that the accounting records 'balance'.

    B   a statement showing the market value of a firm.

    C   a listing, in a particular format, of the balances brought down remaining in the double-entry accounts after the profit and loss account has been prepared.

    D   a statement showing the market value of assets and liabilities.

8.2 The correct heading for the balance sheet of J. Burton at the end of December 1997 is 'Balance Sheet of J. Burton . . .

    A   for the period ended 31 December 1997'.

    B   for the year ended 31 December 1997'.

    C   as at 31 December 1997'.

    D   as at December 1997'.

8.3 The balance sheet of a firm as at any particular date is intended to show . . .

    A   the nature of the firm's business at that date.

    B   the identity of the firm's owners at that date.

    C   the financial position of the firm at that date.

    D   the physical size of the firm at that date.

8.4 A firm's fixed assets are . . .

    A   all of its assets which have a long life and a substantial value.

    B   all of its assets which have an expected useful economic life of more than one year and were purchased in order to be used in the firm on a continuing basis rather than solely for resale.

    C   all assets which have a physical substance.

    D   None of the above.

8.5 A firm's current assets are . . .

- A amounts which it is due to receive within one year of its balance sheet date.
- B its cash and positive bank balances and other assets likely to be converted into cash or bank balances within one year of its balance sheet date as a result of its normal trading operations.
- C the total of its debtors, its stocks and its cash and bank balances.
- D amounts which it is due to receive as a result of credit sales made by it within the last year.

8.6 When preparing a firm's balance sheet, which of the following should be classified as a long-term liability?

- A An amount payable by the firm within six months of the date of the balance sheet.
- B An amount payable by the firm within nine months of the date of the balance sheet.
- C An amount payable by the firm after more than one year from the balance sheet date.
- D None of the above.

8.7 A firm's current liabilities, at its balance sheet date, are . . .

- A its bank overdrafts, if any, and any portions of its term loans which it is due to repay within one year of that date.
- B all liabilities which it is due to discharge within one year of that date.
- C any trade creditors which it is due to pay within three months of that date.
- D all liabilities which it incurred in the six months prior to that date.

8.8 Categorise the three items below as either 'Current liabilities' or 'Long-term liabilities' of a firm as at 31 December 1996 and choose the option A, B, C or D which correctly categorises all three items.

Item 1
A bank loan repayable by the firm as a single lump sum on 31 March 1998.

Item 2
An electricity bill relating to November and December 1996 but unpaid as at 31 December 1996, because the bill was not received by the firm until 10 January 1997, at which time it was recorded in the appropriate ledger accounts.

Item 3
The portion of a five year bank loan due to be paid by the firm in 1997. The loan was taken out on 1 January 1995 and is repayable in equal annual instalments over the term of the loan.

	Item 1	Item 2	Item 3
A	Current	Current	Long-term
B	Current	Long-term	Current
C	Long-term	Current	Long-term
D	Long-term	Current	Current

8.9 The following information relates to a sole trader.

Total of all assets at 1 June	£ 2,300
Total of all liabilities at 1 June	2,500
Net profit earned during June	1,000
Drawings during June	700
Capital introduced during June	5,000

The sole trader's capital at 30 June was:

- A £5,100
- B £5,300
- C £5,500
- D £5,600

8.10 Which of the following summarised balance sheets is correct ?

	Firm 1	Firm 2	Firm 3
Current Assets	£ 100	£ 2,517	£ 2,781
Capital	1,068	2,000	719
Long-term Loan	Nil	500	300
Current Liabilities	375	1,315	950
Fixed Assets	440	1,298	812

- A Firm 1
- B Firm 2
- C Firm 3
- D None of the above.

8.11 A sole trader's capital at any particular date is equal to . . .

- A the sum of his fixed assets plus his current assets at that date.
- B the total of his fixed assets at that date.
- C the total of his net assets at that date plus the total amount of capital he has introduced.
- D the total of his net assets at that date.

8.12 A firm which sells exclusively on credit has the four current assets listed below. Which of the lists shows these assets in decreasing order of liquidity i.e. starting on the left with the most liquid (most readily convertible into cash) of the four and ending on the right with the least liquid (least readily convertible into cash)?

    A   Cash, Stock, Debtors, Money in a bank current account

    B   Money in a bank current account, Cash, Debtors, Stock

    C   Cash, Money in a bank current account, Stock, Debtors

    D   Cash, Money in a bank current account, Debtors, Stock

8.13 On 1 January a sole trader had capital of £25,000. During the year, he withdrew £23,000 for his own use and, at 31 December, he had capital of £31,000. If he did not introduce any new capital during the year, his net profit for the year was:

    A   £17,000

    B   £23,000

    C   £29,000

    D   £32,000

8.14 Which of the following pairs of events would increase the capital of a firm ?

    A   An increase in the firm's fixed assets and a corresponding decrease in its current assets.

    B   An increase in the firm's fixed assets and a corresponding increase in its liabilities.

    C   A decrease in the firm's current assets and no change in its liabilities.

    D   An increase in the firm's assets and a smaller increase in its liabilities.

Section 9

Trading and Profit and Loss Accounts and Balance Sheets: Further Considerations

*If you have difficulty with any of the questions in this section, you should refer to Chapter 9 of **Frank Wood's Business Accounting 1** (Seventh edition)*

9.1 Carriage inwards is included in the cost of sales calculation because . . .

    A   it is a cost associated with the purchase of goods.

    B   it should not be shown in the balance sheet.

    C   carriage outwards is shown as an expense in the profit and loss account.

    D   None of the above.

9.2 The following information concerns a retailing firm.

Sales during July	£ 8,200
Purchases during July	6,400
Stock at 1 July	1,300
Stock at 31 July	900
Carriage inwards on July purchases	200

The firm's cost of sales for July is . . .

    A   £6,200

    B   £6,800

    C   £7,000

    D   None of the above.

9.3 The cost incurred by a firm of bringing goods to a merchantable condition should be included in . . .

    A   its trading account.

    B   its profit and loss account.

    C   its balance sheet.

    D   None of the above.

9.4 The following data relates to a firm which has been trading for several years.

	1996	1995
Sales	£ 1,000,000	£ 900,000
Cost of Sales	500,000	480,000
Stock at 31 December	200,000	150,000

Assuming that the firm's cost of sales is calculated by reference to its purchases and stock figures only, the total of its purchases during 1996 was:

    A   £100,000

    B   £170,000

    C   £450,000

    D   £550,000

9.5 A sole trader incurred a loss of £10,000 during his most recent accounting period, yet had more money in his bank account at the end of the period than he had at the beginning of it. Which of the following, on its own, could explain this ?

    A   An increase in the amount of his stock over the course of the period.

    B   The introduction of £15,000 new capital during the period.

    C   His customers taking longer than normal to pay the amounts they owe to him.

    D   The purchase of fixed assets during the period.

9.6 The correct way to record stock taken by the proprietor of a firm for his own personal use, without him paying for it, is . . .

	Account to Debit	Account to Credit
A	Drawings	Sales
B	Drawings	Stock
C	Sales	Drawings
D	Drawings	Purchases

9.7 The proprietor of a firm took some of the firm's stock for his own use without paying for it. As he considered this to be his 'right', he did not record this transaction. The result of this is that, when final accounts are prepared for the firm, . . .

    A   both its net profit and its closing stock will be overstated.

    B   its net profit will be understated and its closing stock will be unaffected.

    C   both its net profit and its closing stock will be understated.

    D   its net profit will be overstated and its closing stock will be unaffected.

9.8 If, in the accounts of a sole trader, £2,500 was debited to the purchases account, instead of being debited to the drawings account . . .

    A   gross profit would be overstated.

    B   the total of expenses would be understated.

    C   net profit would be understated.

    D   capital would be understated.

9.9 Tom set up a business on 1 January.

He bought fixed assets costing £53,000 and stock costing £6,600. He had financed these in advance of commencing business with a personal loan of £25,000 from his brother and a business loan from a bank. On 31 December of the same year his net assets totalled £37,200. His net profit for the year was £21,100.

Tom's drawings during the year were:

    A   £1,300

    B   £8,900

    C   £16,100

    D   £18,500

9.10 The value of a firm's stock at the end of an accounting period is found by . . .

    A   stocktaking.

    B   looking in the stock account in the nominal (general) ledger.

    C   deducting the total of the firm's purchases from that of its sales.

    D   deducting the firm's cost of sales from the total of its sales.

Section 10

Accounting Concepts

*If you have difficulty with any of the questions in this section, you should refer to Chapter 10 of **Frank Wood's Business Accounting 1** (Seventh edition)*

10.1 When preparing the financial statements of an entity, the going concern concept should be applied, only if the entity concerned . . .

    A   is not expected to incur losses in the foreseeable future.

    B   will never be wound up.

    C   is expected to continue in operational existence for the foreseeable future at a level of activity not significantly less than its current level of activity.

    D   is not expected to be able to continue operating.

10.2 The going concern concept means that, when preparing accounts, . . .

    A   profit should not be anticipated and losses should be provided for as soon as they are foreseen.

    B   items should normally be accounted for in a manner consistent with the way in which they were accounted for in previous years.

    C   unless there is specific information to the contrary, the firm for which the accounts are being prepared should be assumed to continue in operational existence for the foreseeable future at a level of activity not significantly less than the current level of activity.

    D   revenues and costs are recognised as they are earned or incurred, not as money is received or paid.

10.3 The entity concept means that . . .

    A   because a firm is separate and distinct from its owners, those owners cannot have access to its assets unless the firm ceases to trade.

    B   accounts must be prepared for every firm.

    C   the financial affairs of a firm and its owner(s) are always kept separate for the purpose of preparing accounts.

    D   None of the above.

10.4 The effect of the accruals concept is that . . .

    A   similar items should be accounted for in a similar way from one accounting period to the next.

    B   revenue and profit should not be anticipated.

    C   net profit is the difference between revenues and expenses.

    D   None of the above.

10.5 The accruals concept . . .

    A   applies to revenues and expenses only.

    B   applies to assets and liabilities only.

    C   applies to revenues, expenses, assets and liabilities.

    D   is not a fundamental accounting concept.

10.6 An accounting period is . . .

    A   any period for which an entity chooses to prepare its accounts.

    B   a calendar year.

    C   any twelve-month period.

    D   None of the above.

10.7 The effect of the prudence concept is that . . .

    A   net profit is the difference between revenues and expenses rather than the difference between receipts and payments.

    B   losses should be provided for as soon as they are foreseen and profit should not be recorded prematurely.

    C   similar items should be treated in a consistent way from one accounting period to the next.

    D   None of the above.

10.8 The consistency concept means that . . .

    A   when preparing the accounts of a firm, one should normally account for similar items in the same way from one accounting period to the next.

    B   firms in the same industry must account for similar items in the same way.

    C   firms may never change the way in which they prepare their accounts.

    D   None of the above.

10.9 Which of the following is one of the 'fundamental accounting concepts' referred to in SSAP 2 ?

    A   The materiality concept.

    B   The business entity concept.

    C   The going concern concept.

    D   The money measurement concept.

10.10 According to SSAP 2 . . .

    A   the financial statements of a firm must always be prepared on the basis that the firm is a going concern.

    B   materiality is a 'fundamental' accounting concept.

    C   when two or more accounting concepts conflict, the prudence concept overrides the other concept(s).

    D   None of the above.

10.11 Which of the four fundamental accounting concepts (listed below) is sometimes referred to as the matching concept . . .

    A   the accruals concept.

    B   the prudence concept.

    C   the going concern concept.

    D   the consistency concept.

Section 11
Books of Original Entry and Ledgers

If you have difficulty with any of the questions in this section, you should refer to Chapter 11 of **Frank Wood's Business Accounting 1** *(Seventh edition)*

11.1 Which of the following is a 'Book of Original Entry' ?

    A   The sales (debtors) ledger.

    B   The purchases journal (daybook).

    C   The general (nominal) ledger.

    D   The purchases (creditors) ledger.

11.2 Which of the following are entered in the Purchases Journal (otherwise known as the Purchases Daybook) ?

    A   Payments to suppliers.

    B   Trade discount.

    C   Invoices received from suppliers.

    D   Cash discount (also known as settlement discount) received.

11.3 Which of the following is a personal account?

    A   Buildings.

    B   Wages.

    C   Debtors.

    D   None of the above.

11.4 The nominal ledger (also known as the general ledger) is . . .

    A   the 'book' from which the trial balance is extracted.

    B   a 'book of original entry'.

    C   the 'book' in which transactions are first recorded.

    D   None of the above.

11.5 'Posting' means . . .

    A   making the first record of transactions.

    B   recording transactions in a book of original entry.

    C   transferring the total(s) of a book of original entry to the nominal (general) ledger.

    D   None of the above.

Section 12

The Banking System

If you have difficulty with any of the questions in this section, you should refer to Chapter 12 of **Frank Wood's Business Accounting 1** *(Seventh edition)*

12.1 A current account is . . .

    A   a bank account on which cheques can be drawn.

    B   a bank account on which cheques cannot be drawn.

    C   a bank account which does not pay interest.

    D   None of the above.

12.2 A deposit account is . . .

    A   a bank account which pays interest.

    B   a bank account on which cheques can be drawn.

    C   a bank account which does not pay interest.

    D   None of the above.

12.3 A cheque . . .

    A   is the form which must be completed when lodging money into a bank account.

    B   must always be 'crossed'.

    C   is an instruction to your bank to pay money out of your current account.

    D   None of the above.

12.4 Cheques are sometimes 'crossed' . . .

    A   so that they cannot be 'cashed' for a certain period of time.

    B   to prevent them from being lodged into a bank account.

    C   so as to avoid any person, other than the person to whom they are written, deriving any benefit from them.

    D   None of the above.

12.5 Endorsing a cheque means . . .

    A   making it void.

    B   exchanging it for cash at a bank.

    C   relinquishing your right to receive the amount of the cheque and passing that right on to someone else.

    D   None of the above.

12.6 A paying-in slip is . . .

    A   a once-off instruction to a bank to pay a specified amount from your current account.

    B   the form which must be completed when lodging money into a bank account.

    C   the same as a cheque.

    D   None of the above.

12.7 The 'drawer' of a cheque is . . .

    A   The bank in which the person writing the cheque has his / her account.

    B   The person to whom the cheque is written.

    C   The person who writes the cheque or on whose account the cheque is written.

    D   None of the above.

12.8 The payee of a cheque is . . .

    A   The bank in which the person writing the cheque has his / her account.

    B   The person to whom the cheque is written.

    C   The person who writes the cheque or on whose account the cheque is written.

    D   None of the above.

12.9 A bank overdraft . . .

    A   is an asset.

    B   can exist on either a deposit account or a current account.

    C   means that more money has been paid out of a bank current account than has been lodged into it.

    D   None of the above.

Section 13

Cash Books

If you have difficulty with any of the questions in this section, you should refer to Chapter 13 of **Frank Wood's Business Accounting 1** *(Seventh edition)*

13.1 An employee of a video store went to a bank and lodged the previous night's takings, held overnight in the firm's safe.

This transaction should be recorded in the store's Cash Book as:

	Column to Debit	*Column to Credit*
A	Cash	Bank
B	Bank	Cash
C	Cash	Cash
D	Bank	Bank

13.2 A £200 credit balance brought down in the cash columns of a firm's cash book means that . . .

    A   the firm has spent £200 more cash than it has received.

    B   the firm has £200 cash in hand.

    C   a mistake has been made in the recording of cash.

    D   someone has stolen £200 cash.

13.3 A £100 debit balance brought down in the cash column of a firm's Cash Book means that . . .

    A   the firm has £100 cash in hand.

    B   the amount of cash paid out exceeds the amount of cash received by £100.

    C   the total of cash paid out is £100.

    D   the total of cash received is £100.

13.4 Cash discount allowed (also known as settlement discount allowed) to a customer means that the customer is entitled to pay less than the full amount he owes . . .

    A   only if payment is made within an agreed time period.

    B   only if payment is made in cash, not by cheque.

    C   only if payment is made either in cash or by cheque.

    D   only if goods, or other items, are purchased for cash, not on credit.

13.5 Cash discount (also known as settlement discount) received is . . .

    A   deducted from the amount payable by debtors when money is received from them.

    B   given by a firm to its customers when it sells goods on credit.

    C   deducted by a firm when it pays its creditors.

    D   None of the above.

13.6 The total of the discount allowed column in the cash book should be posted to . . .

    A   the debit side of the discount allowed account.

    B   the debit side of the discount received account.

    C   the credit side of the discount allowed account.

    D   the credit side of the discount received account.

Section 14

The Sales Journal and the Sales Ledger

If you have difficulty with any of the questions in this section, you should refer to Chapter 14 of **Frank Wood's Business Accounting 1** *(Seventh edition)*

14.1 The Sales Journal is commonly known as . . .

    A   a sales invoice.

    B   the sales daybook.

    C   the sales ledger.

    D   None of the above.

14.2 The Sales Daybook is used to record . . .

    A   money received from debtors.

    B   the names, addresses, credit terms and other details regarding debtors.

    C   invoices issued to customers in respect of goods sold on credit.

    D   None of the above.

14.3 The total of the Sales Journal is posted to . . .

    A   the credit side of the sales account in the nominal (general) ledger.

    B   the debit side of the sales account in the nominal (general) ledger.

    C   the debit side of the sales daybook.

    D   None of the above.

Section 15

The Purchases Journal and the Purchases Ledger

If you have difficulty with any of the questions in this section, you should refer to Chapter 15 of **Frank Wood's Business Accounting 1** *(Seventh edition)*

15.1 The Purchases Daybook is a record of data extracted from which of the following source documents ?

    A   Invoices received from suppliers.

    B   Invoices issued to customers.

    C   Cheques issued.

    D   Orders received from customers.

15.2 The total of the purchase invoices recorded in the Purchases Journal is posted to . . .

    A   the credit side of the purchases account in the general ledger.

    B   the debit side of the purchases daybook.

    C   the credit side of the purchases daybook.

    D   the debit side of the purchases account in the general ledger.

15.3 A firm which purchased five items on credit at a cost of £80 each, less 25% trade discount, is entitled to deduct a cash discount of 5% if it pays for them, in full, within 14 days of the invoice date.

If the firm pays within the above two-week period, it will have to pay:

    A   £260

    B   £280

    C   £285

    D   None of the above.

Section 16

The Returns Journals

If you have difficulty with any of the questions in this section, you should refer to Chapter 16 of **Frank Wood's Business Accounting 1** *(Seventh edition).*

16.1 Credit notes issued by a firm should initially be recorded in . . .

    A   the sales account in its nominal (general) ledger.

    B   the returns inwards account in its nominal (general) ledger.

    C   the returns inwards journal.

    D   the returns outwards journal.

16.2 The data entered in the Returns Outwards Journal comes from . . .

    A   invoices sent to customers.

    B   invoices received from suppliers.

    C   credit notes sent to customers.

    D   credit notes received from suppliers.

16.3 A wholesaler sold 55 items to a retailer at a price of £20 each, less 20% trade discount. The retailer subsequently returned twelve of the items. As a result of this, the retailer should be sent a credit note for:

    A   £172

    B   £192

    C   £240

    D   £288

16.4 The total of all credit notes received by a firm during a particular period and recorded in its Returns Outwards Journal for that period should be posted to . . .

    A   the credit side of the returns outwards account in its nominal (general) ledger.

    B   the debit side of the returns outwards account in its nominal (general) ledger.

    C   the credit side of the purchases account in its nominal (general) ledger.

    D   the debit side of the purchases account in its nominal (general) ledger.

16.5 The total of credit notes issued to customers recorded in the Returns Inwards Journal is posted to . . .

    A   the debit side of the returns inwards account in the nominal (general) ledger.

    B   the credit side of the sales account in the nominal (general) ledger.

    C   the debit side of the sales account in the nominal (general) ledger.

    D   the credit side of the returns inwards account in the nominal (general) ledger.

Section 17

The Journal

If you have difficulty with any of the questions in this section, you should refer to Chapter 17 of **Frank Wood's Business Accounting 1** *(Seventh edition)*

17.1 The Journal is . . .

    A   part of the double-entry system of accounting.

    B   used to record cash transactions only.

    C   not part of the double-entry accounting system.

    D   None of the above.

17.2 Which of the following should be recorded in the Journal ?

    A   Cash sales.

    B   Fixtures bought on credit.

    C   Goods sold on credit.

    D   None of the above.

Section 18

The Analytical Petty Cash Book and the Imprest System

If you have difficulty with any of the questions in this section, you should refer to Chapter 18 of **Frank Wood's Business Accounting 1** *(Seventh edition)*

18.1 If small cash payments are initially recorded in a Petty Cash Book, rather than being recorded directly into the general ledger, there will be . . .

    A   more entries in the general ledger.

    B   fewer entries in the general ledger.

    C   the same number of entries in the general ledger.

    D   no entries in the general ledger in respect of petty cash.

18.2 During the month of March, a firm which wishes to maintain a petty cash float of £200, paid £146 out of petty cash. How much should it reimburse to the imprest at the end of the month?

    A   £54

    B   £146

    C   £200

    D   £254

Section 19

Value Added Tax

If you have difficulty with any of the questions in this section, you should refer to Chapter 19 of **Frank Wood's Business Accounting 1** *(Seventh edition)*

19.1 The abbreviation 'VAT' means . . .

    A   Variable Agricultural Tax.

    B   Value Associated Tax.

    C   Value Added Tax.

    D   None of the above.

19.2 Value Added Tax . . .

    A   is paid by the purchaser of goods and services, at the relevant rate, on the value added to them by their seller.

    B   is collected by the Inland Revenue on behalf of the government as value is added to goods and services.

    C   is charged at the relevant rate by the sellers of goods and services on the value added by them.

    D   None of the above.

19.3 The standard rate of VAT is:

    A   10%

    B   12.5%

    C   17.5%

    D   21%

19.4 Which of the following statements best describes the treatment of VAT in the accounts of a VAT-registered firm ?

    A   VAT is an expense arising from the sale of goods and services.

    B   VAT is normally a liability, calculated by reference to the purchases and sales of goods, services and other items.

    C   VAT is levied on customers and is payable by them to the Customs and Excise Department.

    D   VAT is collected by firms from their customers and is retained by the firms.

19.5 A person is not obliged to register for VAT unless he has reason to believe that the total taxable turnover of his business activities will exceed, or has exceeded, the current registration limits . . .

    A   in any continuous twelve-month period.

    B   in the next two-month VAT period.

    C   in the twelve months ended on the previous 31 December.

    D   in the most recent two-month VAT period.

19.6 If a firm produces only one product, product X, which is zero-rated for VAT purposes, then . . .

    A   VAT is payable by the firm on its sales of product X and VAT is recoverable by it on its purchases of raw materials used in the production of product X.

    B   VAT is not payable by the firm on its sales of product X and VAT paid on purchases of raw materials used in the production of product X is recoverable.

    C   VAT is not payable by the firm on its sales of product X and VAT is not recoverable on its purchases of raw materials used in the production of product X.

    D   None of the above.

19.7 A firm which sells goods, all of which are exempt from VAT . . .

    A   cannot be charged VAT by any of its suppliers.

    B   cannot be charged VAT by those who supply services to it.

    C   is charged VAT by its suppliers, but may reclaim all of this VAT from the Customs and Excise Department.

    D   is charged VAT by its suppliers and cannot recover all of this VAT from the Customs and Excise Department.

19.8 VAT paid by a taxable person on the purchase of goods and / or services, other than goods or services in respect of which VAT cannot be reclaimed, from another taxable person is known as . . .

    A   output credits.

    B   input credits.

    C   irrecoverable VAT.

    D   None of the above.

19.9 If the total of sales, including VAT at the rate of 10%, amounts to £1,800, the total of sales excluding VAT amounts to:

    A   £1,620

    B   £1,636

    C   £1,720

    D   None of the above.

19.10 The amount of VAT included in goods costing £200, inclusive of VAT at the rate of 21%, is:

    A   £31.50

    B   £34.71

    C   £42.00

    D   None of the above.

19.11 A VAT-registered sole trader has the following VAT-inclusive transactions for a two-month VAT period.

Sales	£ 11,000
Purchases for re-sale	5,500
Other purchases	1,100

If the rate of VAT is 10%, all sales are liable to VAT and VAT can be reclaimed on all purchases, the sole trader's VAT liability for the period is:

    A   £340

    B   £390

    C   £400

    D   £440

19.12 A VAT-registered car dealer allows a customer £6,500 (including VAT at the rate of 21%) for his used car as a trade-in against a new car, the retail price of which is £15,000 (including VAT at the rate of 21%). As a result of this transaction, the car dealer is liable to pay VAT of:

    A   £1,475.21

    B   £1,785.00

    C   £3,150.00

    D   None of the above.

19.13 In the Profit and Loss Account of a VAT-registered firm, the sales figure . . .

    A   should be exclusive of any VAT charged on sales.

    B   should exclude cash sales.

    C   should exclude credit sales.

    D   None of the above.

19.14 Irrecoverable VAT on the purchase of fixed assets should be . . .

    A   shown as an expense in the profit and loss account for the period in which the asset is purchased.

    B   shown as part of the cost of fixed assets in the balance sheet.

    C   deducted from any VAT payable on sales.

    D   None of the above.

19.15 During an accounting period, a VAT-registered firm incurred advertising expenditure totalling £12,500, including VAT at the rate of 25%. The charge for advertising which should be shown in the firm's profit and loss account for the same period is:

    A   £9,375

    B   £10,000

    C   £15,000

    D   £15,625

19.16 The payment by a firm of its VAT liability for a taxable period should initially be recorded in its:

    A   journal.

    B   cash book (or cheque payments book).

    C   sales daybook.

    D   None of the above.

19.17 A firm, which is registered for VAT, purchased plant and machinery costing £12,100 (including recoverable VAT at the rate of 21%) on credit. The figures that will be shown in the balance sheet in relation to this transaction are:

	Plant & Machinery	VAT	Creditors
A	£12,100 Dr.	-	£12,100 Cr.
B	£9,680 Dr.	£2,420 Dr.	£12,100 Cr.
C	£10,000 Dr.	£2,100 Dr.	£12,100 Cr.
D	£10,000 Dr.	-	£10,000 Cr.

19.18 If, for any given accounting period, the total of the debit entries in a firm's VAT account equals that of the credit entries, thus leaving no balance on the account at the end of the period . . .

    A   the firm is not a VAT-registered firm.

    B   the firm deals exclusively in goods and / or services which are exempt from VAT.

    C   the firm does not owe any VAT to the Customs and Excise Department at that date.

    D   None of the above.

19.19 A debit balance brought down on the VAT account in a firm's nominal (general) ledger represents:

    A   an expense.

    B   VAT payable to the Customs and Excise Department.

    C   irrecoverable VAT.

    D   VAT recoverable from the Customs and Excise Department.

19.20 At the beginning of a VAT period, a firm which buys and sells exclusively on credit owed £2,000 to the Customs and Excise Department in respect of VAT. Its credit sales and credit purchases for the period, inclusive of VAT at the rate of 20%, amounted to £72,000 and £48,000 respectively. During the period the firm paid £3,000 to the Customs and Excise Department in respect of VAT.

What was the balance carried down on the firm's VAT account at the end of the period ?

    A   £3,000 Debit

    B   £3,000 Credit

    C   £3,400 Debit

    D   £3,900 Credit

19.21 A form 'VAT 100' is . . .

    A   the form used by firms to register for VAT.

    B   a form issued by the Customs and Excise Department demanding immediate payment of VAT outstanding.

    C   the form on which periodic VAT returns are made by VAT-registered firms.

    D   None of the above.

Section 20

Columnar Day Books

If you have difficulty with any of the questions in this section, you should refer to Chapter 20 of **Frank Wood's Business Accounting 1** *(Seventh edition)*

20.1 Which of the following types of firm need not include an analysis column for VAT in its columnar sales book (sales analysis book) ?

    A   a VAT registered business.

    B   a business which buys only zero-rated goods and services and sells goods which are liable to VAT at the rate of 10%.

    C   a business which has not registered for VAT because its turnover is below the relevant exemption limit.

    D   None of the above.

Section 21

Employees' Pay

If you have difficulty with any of the questions in this section, you should refer to Chapter 21 of ***Frank Wood's Business Accounting 1*** *(Seventh edition)*

21.1 An employee, whose annual salary is £24,000 and who has a tax-free allowance of £8,000 for the current tax year, pays PAYE at the rate of 48%.

The amount of PAYE that will be deducted from his salary for the year is:

- A £7,680
- B £11,520
- C £16,000
- D None of the above.

21.2 When preparing the financial statements of a firm, PAYE deducted by the firm from its employees' gross pay and not yet remitted to the Inland Revenue should . . .

- A be shown only as an expense in the profit and loss account.
- B be shown as a liability in the balance sheet.
- C be deducted from the wages expense which would otherwise be shown in the profit and loss account.
- D None of the above.

21.3 Any balance on the PAYE account in the nominal (general) ledger at the end of an accounting period represents . . .

- A the PAYE expense for that period.
- B the amount of PAYE paid during the period.
- C the cumulative amount of PAYE deducted from employees which has not yet been paid to the Inland Revenue.
- D None of the above.

21.4 Employers must remit to the Inland Revenue PAYE deducted from their employees for the month ended 5 April on or before . . .

- A 14 April.
- B 19 April.
- C 30 April.
- D None of the above.

21.5 The end-of-year PAYE / National Insurance return for a tax year (ended on 5 April) should be submitted to the Inland Revenue by . . .

    A   14 April.

    B   19 April.

    C   30 April.

    D   None of the above.

Section 22

Computers and Accounting

If you have difficulty with any of the questions in this section, you should refer to Chapter 22 of **Frank Wood's Business Accounting 1** *(Seventh edition)*

22.1 The abbreviation 'LAN' means . . .

    A   Local Accounting Network.

    B   Local Area Network.

    C   Large Accounting Network.

    D   None of the above.

22.2 The abbreviation 'AIS' means . . .

    A   Accounting Information Service.

    B   Accounting Information System.

    C   Accounting Intelligence System.

    D   None of the above.

22.3 The abbreviation 'MIS' means . . .

    A   Management Information System.

    B   Management Intelligence Service.

    C   Management Information Service.

    D   None of the above.

Section 23

Depreciation of Fixed Assets: Nature and Calculations

If you have difficulty with any of the questions in this section, you should refer to Chapter 23 of **Frank Wood's Business Accounting 1** *(Seventh edition)*

23.1 Depreciation is . . .

    A   a way of setting aside money to provide for the eventual replacement of fixed assets.

    B   a way of writing off the cost of fixed assets over their estimated revenue-generating period.

    C   the writing off of the cost of fixed assets evenly over their estimated useful economic lives.

    D   the writing off of the cost of fixed assets over their estimated useful economic lives in ever decreasing amounts.

23.2 The purpose of charging depreciation as an expense in the profit and loss account is . . .

    A   to allocate the cost of acquiring fixed assets over the accounting periods expected to benefit from their use.

    B   to ensure that funds will be available for the eventual replacement of fixed assets.

    C   to reduce the figure shown in the balance sheet for fixed assets from the cost of those fixed assets to their estimated market value.

    D   to comply with the prudence concept.

23.3 The depreciation charge shown in the profit and loss account . . .

    A   is a revenue expense.

    B   is capital expenditure.

    C   can be either capital expenditure or a revenue expense, depending on the nature of the fixed asset being depreciated.

    D   None of the above.

23.4 'Obsolescence' means . . .

    A   the decline in the value of fixed assets as a result of them becoming outdated by technological improvement and invention.

    B   the decline in the book value of fixed assets as a result of them being depreciated using the straight-line method of depreciation.

    C   the decline in the book value of fixed assets as a result of them being depreciated using the reducing balance method of depreciation.

    D   None of the above.

23.5 SSAP 12 . . .

   A   specifies that the straight line method of depreciation must always be used.

   B   specifies that the reducing balance method of depreciation must always be used.

   C   allows either the straight line method or the reducing balance method of depreciation to be used provided that only one of them is used in any particular accounting period.

   D   does not specify that any particular method of depreciation must be used at any time.

23.6 A business which owns all of its fixed assets should normally depreciate . . .

   A   all of its fixed assets.

   B   all of its fixed assets which are of significant value.

   C   all of its fixed assets except freehold land.

   D   all of its fixed assets except land.

23.7 If the depreciation on a fixed asset is calculated by reference to the reducing balance method . . .

   A   then, in relation to that particular fixed asset, there will be an equal depreciation charge in the profit and loss account of each year during the life of the asset.

   B   the depreciation charge in the profit and loss account in respect of that asset will decrease each year over the life of the asset.

   C   the depreciation charge in the profit and loss account relating to that asset will be greater in the later years of the life of the asset than in the earlier years.

   D   all other things being equal, net profit will be greater in the earlier years of the life of the asset than in the later years.

23.8 The net book value of a fixed asset, other then freehold land, which has not been revalued, is . . .

   A   the amount it cost to acquire it.

   B   the amount it would cost to buy it, or a similar asset, now.

   C   the amount it cost to acquire it less the aggregate (total) depreciation charged on it.

   D   the amount it cost to acquire it less its estimated scrap value.

23.9 A firm bought a machine for £33,000. It expects to use the machine for eleven years and then sell it for £11,000. If the firm calculates depreciation by reference to the straight-line method, the annual depreciation charge, in respect of this machine, will be:

   A   £1,000

   B   £2,000

   C   £2,500

   D   £3,000

23.10 A firm bought a fixed asset for £500,000. The asset has an estimated useful economic life of ten years and an estimated scrap value of £50,000.

If the asset is depreciated at the rate of 20% per annum, using the reducing balance method, the depreciation charge, in relation to this asset alone, in the second year of its life will be:

- A £45,000
- B £72,000
- C £80,000
- D £90,000

23.11 A firm owns fixed assets which, in total, cost £200,000. Aggregate depreciation on these assets amounts to £80,000. If the firm depreciates its fixed assets at the rate of 20% per annum, using the straight-line method, the depreciation charge in its profit and loss account for the current accounting period is:

- A £16,000
- B £20,000
- C £24,000
- D £40,000

23.12 A firm depreciates its productive plant and equipment at the rate of 10% per annum, using the reducing balance method. It is the firm's policy to charge a full year's depreciation on fixed assets in the year in which they are acquired.

Given the above, what is the depreciation charge, to the nearest pound, to be shown in the 1995 accounts in relation to an item of plant, with no residual value, acquired in 1991 for £10,000 ?

- A £591
- B £656
- C £729
- D £1,000

23.13 The following information relates to one of several fixed assets acquired by a firm on 1 January 1996.

Cost	£ 29,800
Estimated scrap value	£ 5,000
Estimated useful economic life	8 years

If all of the firm's fixed assets are depreciated at the rate of 20% per annum, using the reducing balance method, the total depreciation charged on the above asset up to 31 December 2003 will be:

- A £4,960
- B £5,960
- C £24,800
- D £29,800

23.14 A firm's financial year-end is 31 December. Its plant and equipment consists of the following machines.

Machine	Cost	Date of Purchase
1	£10,000	1 January 1993
2	£8,000	1 July 1993
3	£14,000	1 April 1995

The firm provides for depreciation of its plant and equipment at the rate of 10% per annum on a strict time basis, using the reducing balance method. The depreciation charge on plant and equipment in the firm's accounts for 1996 was:

    A   £2,639.60

    B   £2,672.40

    C   £3,095.00

    D   £3,200.00

23.15 A machine, which was bought at a cost of £3,200 is not expected to have any residual value. If it is depreciated at the rate of 25% per annum, using the reducing balance method, its net book value, after two years, will be:

    A   £1,600

    B   £1,800

    C   £2,400

    D   None of the above.

23.16 A firm depreciates its fixed assets, all of which were purchased on 1 January 1993, at the rate of 25% per annum, using the reducing balance method. If the total depreciation charged on these assets up to 31 December 1995 was £23,125 their net book value at that date was:

    A   £7,708

    B   £10,000

    C   £16,875

    D   £17,500

Section 24

Double-Entry Records for Depreciation

If you have difficulty with any of the questions in this section, you should refer to Chapter 24 of **Frank Wood's Business Accounting 1** *(Seventh edition)*

24.1 If there is a separate provision for depreciation account in the nominal (general) ledger for each category of fixed asset, the double-entry to record the depreciation charge on machinery for the current year is:

	Account to Debit	Account to Credit
A	Profit and loss	Provision for depreciation of machinery
B	Machinery	Profit and loss
C	Profit and loss	Machinery
D	None of the above.	

24.2 Any balance brought down on a provision for depreciation account . . .

    A   should be included in the trial balance as a debit balance.

    B   should be included in the trial balance as a credit balance.

    C   should sometimes be included in the trial balance as a debit balance and sometimes as a credit balance.

    D   should not be included in the trial balance at all.

24.3 If the depreciation charge on vehicles for the current year is accounted for by debiting the profit and loss account and crediting the provision for depreciation of vehicles account, then, after the above entries have been made, the balance on the provision for depreciation of vehicles account is . . .

    A   transferred to the vehicles account.

    B   listed in the trial balance.

    C   deducted from the cost / valuation of vehicles in the balance sheet.

    D   transferred to the profit and loss account.

24.4 Upon the disposal of a vehicle, the double-entry which a furniture retailer should make to record the receipt of the sale proceeds is:

	Account to Debit	Account to Credit
A	Bank	Sales
B	Vehicle disposals	Vehicle
C	Bank	Vehicle disposals
D	Vehicle	Provision for depreciation

24.5 When a machine is disposed of, the correct way to record the total depreciation charged on it up to the date of disposal is:

    A   Debit the Provision for depreciation of machinery account and
Credit the Machinery account.

    B   Debit the Provision for depreciation of machinery account and
Credit the Machinery disposal account.

    C   Debit the Machinery account and
Credit the Provision for depreciation of machinery account.

    D   Debit the Machinery disposal account and
Credit the Provision for depreciation of machinery account.

24.6 A loss incurred upon the disposal of plant and equipment should be . . .

    A   credited to the plant and equipment account.

    B   debited to the profit and loss account.

    C   debited to the provision for depreciation account.

    D   credited to the provision for depreciation account.

24.7 The balance on a firm's plant and machinery account on 1 January 1996 was £5,000. During that year the following transactions took place on the dates shown.

    1 May   Plant, which had originally cost £750, was sold.

    1 September   New machinery costing £3,000 was purchased.

If depreciation is calculated at the rate of 10% per annum, on a strict time basis, using the straight line method, the depreciation charge on plant and machinery for 1996, to the nearest pound, is:

    A   £525

    B   £550

    C   £600

    D   £625

24.8 On 1 January 1993, a firm bought a second-hand van for £6,000 and paid £260 to have the firm's name and logo painted on it.

The firm depreciates vehicles over a five year period using the straight-line method, assuming a nil residual value. A full year's depreciation is charged in the year of acquisition and none in the year of disposal. The firm's accounting year-end is 31 December.

What was the profit on the sale of the van, if it was sold for £5,000 on 31 March 1996 ?

    A   £1,000

    B   £1,244

    C   £2,496

    D   £2,600

24.9 On 31 August 1992 a firm bought a machine for £44,000. At that date, the estimated useful economic life of the machine was seven years and its estimated residual value was £2,000. On 30 June 1996 the firm sold the machine for £18,000. The firm's accounting period-end is 31 December and its policy is to calculate depreciation using the straight line method, charging a full year's depreciation in the year of acquisition and no depreciation in the year of disposal.

The profit earned, or the loss incurred, on the disposal of the machine was:

    A   Loss of £2,000

    B   Loss of £3,000

    C   Loss of £3,500

    D   Profit of £4,000

24.10 On 1 January 1993, a firm, whose financial year-end is 31 December, bought an item of plant for £10,000. Initially, it was decided to depreciate the plant over ten years, using the straight line method, assuming no residual value. On 1 January 1995, it became apparent that the plant would last only another five years, over which period it would be used equally.

The depreciation charge for 1995 in respect of the above item was:

    A   £1,000

    B   £1,429

    C   £1,600

    D   £2,000

24.11 On 1 January 1993, a firm bought a machine for £4,200. At that date, the machine's useful economic life was estimated to be seven years and its scrap value was estimated to be zero. On 1 January 1995 the machine's useful economic life was re-estimated to be five years in total and its scrap value was re-estimated to be £300.

If the straight line method of depreciation was used to depreciate the machine, the depreciation charged on it for 1995 was:

    A   £540

    B   £780

    C   £840

    D   £900

24.12 On 1 April 1991, a firm bought a machine for £420,000. At that date, the machine had an expected useful economic life of five years and an expected residual value of £20,000. On 1 April 1995 the firm spent £240,000 on a major refurbishment of the machine which extended its useful life by three years and revised its estimated residual value to £60,000. If the firm uses the straight line method of depreciation, the depreciation charge for this machine, to be included in the accounts for the year ended 31 March 1996, is:

    A   £65,000

    B   £70,000

    C   £80,000

    D   £93,333

Section 25

Capital and Revenue Expenditure

If you have difficulty with any of the questions in this section, you should refer to Chapter 25 of **Frank Wood's Business Accounting 1** *(Seventh edition)*

25.1 All expenditure, when incurred, is shown either as a cost of sale or an expense in the profit and loss account or as a fixed asset in the balance sheet. In deciding where to show the expenditure, which of the following is *not* relevant ?

    A   The improvement value, if any, of the expenditure.

    B   The likelihood of being able to recover the expenditure in future accounting periods.

    C   The date on which the expenditure was incurred.

    D   None of the above.

25.2 Capital expenditure is . . .

    A   money brought into a firm by its proprietor.

    B   expenditure incurred to finance the day-to-day operations of a firm.

    C   expenditure incurred on the acquisition or improvement of fixed assets.

    D   None of the above.

25.3 Which of the following is capital expenditure ?

    A   The cost of repairing a vehicle.

    B   The cost of acquiring a vehicle for re-sale.

    C   Proceeds arising from the sale of a van which had been used in the business to make deliveries to customers.

    D   The cost of a new vehicle acquired for continuing use in the business.

25.4 In the case of a vehicle retailer, which of the following is capital expenditure ?

    A   The annual cost of a computer maintenance contract.

    B   Legal fees relating to employee accident claims.

    C   The cost of constructing a roof over the service station area.

    D   The purchase of vehicles for re-sale.

25.5 Which of the following is revenue expenditure ?

    A   The cost of acquiring machinery for continuing use in the business.

    B   The introduction of additional capital by a proprietor.

    C   The cost of advertising a mid-season sale.

    D   The transfer of surplus funds from a bank current account to a bank deposit account.

25.6 In the case of a newsagent, which of the following is a revenue receipt ?

    A   The proceeds of the sale of plant and equipment.

    B   Money received from an insurance company as a result of crashing a delivery vehicle.

    C   A refund received from a supplier as compensation for damaged stock supplied.

    D   None of the above.

25.7 If, in the case of an engineering firm, the cost of acquiring a vehicle is inadvertently debited to the motor expenses account in the nominal (general) ledger . . .

    A   the total of current assets will be understated.

    B   the total of current liabilities will be overstated.

    C   the total of motor expenses will be understated.

    D   the total of fixed assets will be understated.

Section 26

Bad Debts, Provisions for Bad Debts, Provisions for Discounts on Debtors

*If you have difficulty with any of the questions in this section, you should refer to Chapter 26 of **Frank Wood's Business Accounting 1** (Seventh edition)*

26.1 The rationale for making a provision in respect of doubtful debts is that the provision . . .

    A   is an estimate of future bad debts.

    B   records the expense of bad debts as they are incurred.

    C   matches the estimated cost of future bad debts against the revenue earned in giving rise to the potential bad debts.

    D   records bad debts without taking them out of the 'books' of an entity, thus showing the full amount owed by debtors as a current asset.

26.2 Relative to not having a provision for bad or doubtful debts, the existence of such a provision . . .

    A   increases the total of current liabilities.

    B   reduces the cost of sales.

    C   reduces the total of current assets.

    D   None of the above.

26.3 A credit balance on Mr. Murphy's account in a firm's debtors ledger means that . . .

    A   the amount owed by Murphy is a bad debt.

    B   one or more of Murphy's cheques has 'bounced'.

    C   the firm owes money to Murphy.

    D   a provision should be made specifically against Murphy's account.

26.4 When preparing financial statements, the bad debts account is 'closed' by a transfer to . . .

    A   the balance sheet.

    B   the profit and loss account.

    C   the trading account.

    D   the provision for bad debts account.

26.5 Provision for discount allowed on outstanding debtors balances should be calculated, at an appropriate rate, on . . .

    A   total debtors net of any bad debts written off.

    B   total debtors before account is taken of bad debts.

    C   total debtors less total creditors.

    D   total debtors net of any bad debts written off and after deducting the cumulative amount of any provision for doubtful debts.

Section 27

Other Adjustments for Final Accounts

If you have difficulty with any of the questions in this section, you should refer to Chapter 27 of **Frank Wood's Business Accounting 1** *(Seventh edition)*

27.1 In the balance sheet of a sole trader, accruals should be shown as part of . . .

    A   fixed assets.

    B   drawings.

    C   current assets.

    D   current liabilities.

27.2 In the balance sheet of a sole trader, prepayments should be shown as . . .

    A   a deduction from capital.

    B   part of creditors.

    C   a deduction from current liabilities.

    D   part of current assets.

27.3 In the case of a firm which rents the premises from which it operates, a credit balance brought down on its rent payable account at a particular date, means that, at that date, . . .

    A   the firm owes rent.

    B   the firm has paid rent in advance.

    C   the firm has paid too much rent.

    D   the firm has paid too little rent.

27.4 Expenses relevant to an accounting period which remain unpaid at the end of the period should . . .

    A   be shown as an expense in the profit and loss account for the period and shown as a current liability in the balance sheet at the end of the period.

    B   be shown as an asset in the balance sheet at the end of the period and shown as income in the profit and loss account for the period.

    C   be shown as part of long-term liabilities in the balance sheet at the end of the period.

    D   be netted off against prepayments at the same date and shown together, as a single figure, in the balance sheet at the end of the period.

27.5 The effect of the year-end adjustment required in respect of rates prepaid is . . .

- A to decrease the figures shown in the balance sheet for both creditors and prepayments.
- B to decrease both the rates expense shown in the profit and loss account and the figure shown in the balance sheet for prepayments.
- C to increase the figures shown in the balance sheet for both prepayments and creditors.
- D to increase the figure shown in the balance sheet for prepayments and to decrease the rates expense shown in the profit and loss account.

27.6 Advertising expenditure paid by a firm during its first year in business but relating to a subsequent accounting period should be shown in the financial statements for the current accounting period . . .

- A as a prepayment in the balance sheet and as an expense in the profit and loss account.
- B as a deduction from the figure for bank in the balance sheet and as revenue in the profit and loss account.
- C as a prepayment in the balance sheet and as a deduction from the total of advertising expenditure paid in the profit and loss account.
- D as an accrual in the balance sheet and as revenue in the profit and loss account.

27.7 Which of the following statements is correct ?

- A The accounting concept which gives rise to adjustments at the end of an accounting period in respect of accruals and prepayments is the consistency concept.
- B A prepayment adjustment should be made in respect of each expense which is overpaid at the year-end.
- C Revenue should not be shown in the profit and loss account unless the associated money has been received.
- D None of the above.

27.8 If a £500 salaries accrual was inadvertently treated as a prepayment, net profit would be . . .

- A overstated by £500.
- B understated by £500.
- C overstated by £1,000.
- D understated by £1,000.

27.9 On 1 January 1995, a new firm, whose financial year-end is 31 December, rented premises at a cost of £10,000 per annum, payable quarterly in arrears. Four payments, each of £2,500, were made on 31 March 1995, 2 July 1995, 4 October 1995 and 6 January 1996.

The rent figure in the preliminary trial balance as at 31 December 1995 should be:

    A   £7,500

    B   £10,000

    C   £12,500

    D   £30,000

27.10 During 1994 an employee borrowed £10,000 from the firm where he worked at a simple interest rate of 10% per annum, fixed for the three years over which the loan was to be repaid in equal monthly instalments. On 1 January 1995, the employee had paid £100 interest in advance. On 31 December 1995, the employee was in arrears with his interest payments to the extent of £300. The figure for interest receivable on this loan in the firm's profit and loss account for 1995, is:

    A   £850

    B   £1,000

    C   £1,150

    D   £1,250

27.11 A firm which commenced business on 1 January 1994 rents the premises from which it operates. During 1995 the firm paid rent of £1,320. This was 10% more than the total rent expense for 1994 - only half of which was paid by 31 December 1994. If there is no accrual or prepayment in respect of rent at 31 December 1995 the rent expense for the year then ended is:

    A   £600

    B   £720

    C   £1,200

    D   £1,320

27.12 A sole trader rents the premises from which he operates and does not pay or receive any other rent. On 1 January 1995 the rent account in his ledger showed accrued rent payable of £2,500. During 1995 the trader paid rent totalling £12,750 including all bills in respect of 1995 and one bill for £3,750 in respect of the three months ended on 31 January 1996.

The charge for rent, in the profit and loss account for 1995 was:

    A   £9,000

    B   £11,500

    C   £12,750

    D   £14,000

27.13 During its first financial year, ended on 31 December 1995, a firm paid £3,000 in respect of insurance premiums. All premiums were paid in advance and, except for the following, related to policies with renewal dates similar to the firm's accounting year-end date.

	Policy X	Policy Y
Annual premium	£240	£1,200
Renewal date	30 June 1996	30 April 1996
Premium paid	1 July 1995	1 May 1995

The firm's insurance expense for 1995 was:

- A £2,280
- B £2,480
- C £2,580
- D £3,000

27.14 If rent receivable has been prepaid to the extent of £75 at the end of a firm's first financial year, the amount of rental income shown in its profit and loss account, relative to the amount of rent it received during the year, will be . . .

- A the same.
- B £75 more.
- C £75 less.
- D None of the above.

27.15 A firm records all transactions relating to the expense for both rent and rates in a single ledger account.

On 1 January there was an accrual of £900 in respect of rent and a prepayment of £600 in respect of rates. On 31 December there was a rent accrual of £1,100 and rates prepaid of £700. During the year, £4,800 was paid in respect of rent and £3,100 in respect of rates.

The total expense for both rent and rates for the year is:

- A £7,800
- B £8,000
- C £8,100
- D £8,200

27.16 A firm records all transactions relating to the expense for both rent and rates in a single ledger account.

At the start of the year there was an accrual in respect of rent of £2,500 and a prepayment in respect of rates of £3,000. At the end of the year, there was rent due of £4,500 and rates prepaid of £3,500. The total expense for both rent and rates for the year was £36,000.

The total amount paid during the year, in respect of both rent and rates, was:

    A   £34,500

    B   £35,500

    C   £36,500

    D   £37,500

27.17 A firm records all transactions relating to the expense of both postage and stationery in a single ledger account. At the beginning of a financial year, there is both a debit balance brought down of £50 and a credit balance brought down of £100 on the account. Which of the following alternatives could explain this situation ?

    A   The firm has a stock of stationery worth £50.

    B   Postage is prepaid to the extent of £100.

    C   The firm has a stock of stationery worth £100.

    D   Postage payable amounts to £50.

Section 28

The Valuation of Stock

*If you have difficulty with any of the questions in this section, you should refer to Chapter 28 of **Frank Wood's Business Accounting 1** (Seventh edition)*

28.1 Stock should be included in the balance sheet at . . .

    A   its cost.

    B   its net realisable value.

    C   the lower of its total cost and its total net realisable value.

    D   the lower of its cost and its net realisable value on an item-by-item or category-by-category basis.

28.2 A firm has two categories of stock. The cost and net realisable value (NRV) of each are as follows.

	Cost	NRV
Category 1	£ 35,000	£ 22,000
Category 2	22,000	25,000

The figure to be included in the firm's balance sheet, in respect of stock, is:

    A   £44,000

    B   £47,000

    C   £57,000

    D   £60,000

28.3 The net realisable value of an item of stock is its actual or estimated selling price . . .

    A   plus all further costs to completion and all costs to be incurred in marketing, selling and distributing the item.

    B   less all further costs to completion.

    C   less all further costs to completion and all costs to be incurred in marketing, selling and distributing the item.

    D   None of the above.

28.4 If an item of stock which originally cost £1,420 can be sold for £1,600, after incurring further completion costs of £110 and advertising costs of £130, then it should be included in the balance sheet stock valuation at:

    A   £1,360

    B   £1,420

    C   £1,490

    D   £1,600

28.5 The valuation of stock at the lower of its cost and its net realisable value is an application of . . .

    A   the consistency concept.

    B   the going concern concept.

    C   the prudence concept.

    D   the accruals concept.

28.6 The abbreviation 'FIFO' means . . .

    A   Fixed Income Financial Operations.

    B   Final Interest-Free Option.

    C   The First-In-First-Out method of approximating the cost of stock.

    D   None of the above.

28.7 The abbreviation 'LIFO' means . . .

    A   Large Integrated Financial Organisation.

    B   Least Interesting Financial Option.

    C   The Last-In-First-Out method of approximating the cost of stock.

    D   None of the above.

28.8 According to SSAP 9, which of the following is *not* normally acceptable as a basis for approximating the cost of stock when publishing financial statements ?

    A   The first in, first out (FIFO) method.

    B   The last in, first out (LIFO) method.

    C   The weighted average cost method.

    D   None of the above.

28.9 Under which of the following methods of approximating the cost of stock are the oldest stock costs incurred *unlikely* to have an effect on the closing stock valuation ?

    A   The first in, first out (FIFO) method.

    B   The last in, first out (LIFO) method.

    C   The weighted average cost method.

    D   None of the above.

28.10 If prices fall consistently throughout an accounting period, the method of approximating the cost of stock which will give the highest value to closing stock is:

    A   The first in, first out (FIFO) method.

    B   The last in, first out (LIFO) method.

    C   The weighted average cost method.

    D   None of the above.

28.11 The Last-In-First-Out (LIFO) method of approximating the cost of stock . . .

    A   reflects up-to-date costs in the balance sheet value of stock.

    B   matches revenue with up-to-date costs.

    C   smoothes the effect of fluctuations in purchase prices.

    D   None of the above.

28.12 Which of the following methods of approximating the cost of stock yields a cost of sales figure which most accurately reflects the actual cost of sales under normal circumstances ?

    A   The first in, first out method (FIFO).

    B   The last in, first out method (LIFO).

    C   The weighted average cost method.

    D   None of the above.

28.13 The accounting concept which prevents firms from frequently changing the stock valuation method they use, thereby preventing them from manipulating the figures in their profit and loss accounts and balance sheets, is:

    A   The materiality concept.

    B   The consistency concept.

    C   The prudence concept.

    D   The going concern concept.

28.14 After preparing its profit and loss account for a calendar year, in which it reported a net profit of £20,000, a firm discovered that its stock at 1 January had been under-valued by £2,000 and that its stock at 31 December had been over-valued by £3,000. The firm's reported net profit for the year should have been . . .

    A   £15,000

    B   £19,000

    C   £21,000

    D   £25,000

Section 29

Bank Reconciliation Statements

If you have difficulty with any of the questions in this section, you should refer to Chapter 29 of **Frank Wood's Business Accounting 1** *(Seventh edition)*

29.1 A bank reconciliation statement is a statement which . . .

    A   is sent by banks to their customers.

    B   is sent by banks to any of their customers who exceed their agreed credit limit with the bank.

    C   explains the difference between the bank balance shown in a firm's accounting records and that shown on its bank statement.

    D   None of the above.

29.2 The purpose of a firm preparing a bank reconciliation statement is . . .

    A   to ascertain the amount of financing, if any, which it may require in the future.

    B   to ascertain whether bank charges have been correctly calculated by the bank.

    C   to ascertain whether the correct amount of interest has been paid to the firm by the bank on all money on deposit.

    D   to reconcile the bank balance in the firm's accounting records at a particular date with that shown on its bank statement at the same date.

29.3 A bank reconciliation statement is . . .

    A   part of the double-entry accounting records.

    B   not part of the double-entry accounting records.

    C   prepared by a firm and then sent to its bank.

    D   posted to the nominal (general) ledger.

29.4 A cheque which was issued by a firm and sent to one of its creditors has not yet appeared on the firm's bank statement. This cheque is known as . . .

    A   a standing order.

    B   a dishonoured cheque.

    C   a credit transfer.

    D   an outstanding cheque.

29.5 The figure for 'bank' which should be shown in a firm's balance sheet at any particular date is . . .

    A   the balance, at that date, as shown by the firm's bank statement.

    B   the balance, at that date, per the firm's bank nominal (general) ledger account.

    C   the reconciled bank balance at that date.

    D   None of the above.

29.6 The total of cheques issued during the last six months which, at the date on which a bank reconciliation statement is prepared, have not been shown on the bank statement . . .

    A   should be included in the bank reconciliation statement.

    B   should be shown in the balance sheet under the heading 'accruals'.

    C   should be cancelled.

    D   are 'stale' cheques.

29.7 Which of the following will *not* give rise to a difference between the balance shown on a firm's bank statement and that shown, at the same date, in its nominal (general) ledger account for bank ?

    A   Errors made by the firm's bank.

    B   Cheques written by the firm which have not yet appeared on its bank statement.

    C   Lodgements made by the firm which have not yet appeared on its bank statement.

    D   None of the above.

29.8 If cheques totalling £12,000 sent by a firm to its creditors during an accounting period have not been presented at a bank by the end of that period, then, at that date, on the basis of the above information only . .

    A   the firm is owed £12,000 by its bank.

    B   the bank balance shown in the firm's nominal (general) ledger is overstated by £12,000.

    C   the balance shown on the firm's bank statement is £12,000 greater than the amount the firm has available to it from that bank account.

    D   the firm owes its creditors £12,000 more than the amount which will be shown for creditors in its balance sheet.

29.9 On 31 March the balance brought down on a firm's bank account in its ledger was £3,600, credit. At the same date, outstanding cheques amounted to £1,400 and outstanding lodgements amounted to £2,000. A cheque for £500, received from a debtor, was subsequently dishonoured. The receipt of the cheque had been correctly recorded but no entry has yet been made in the accounting records in respect of it being dishonoured. On the basis of the above information, the balance on the firm's bank statement at 31 March was:

    A   £3,500 credit

    B   £3,700 credit

    C   £4,200 overdrawn

    D   £4,700 overdrawn

29.10 At 31 December the balance on a firm's bank statement was £1,000 overdrawn. At the same date, outstanding cheques amounted to £3,000, outstanding lodgements amounted to £5,000 and there was a dishonoured cheque from a customer of £500 entered on the firm's bank statement but not yet entered in the bank account in the firm's ledger. The balance brought down on the bank account in the firm's ledger was:

    A   £500 debit

    B   £500 credit

    C   £1,000 credit

    D   £1,500 debit

29.11 At 31 May, according to John Smith's creditors' ledger, he owed Alpha Ltd., one of his suppliers, £1,518. The balance shown on the statement he received from Alpha Ltd. did not agree with this. A purchase by John Smith from Alpha Ltd. of goods costing £520 was recorded on Alpha's statement but not in John Smith's ledger. A cheque for £250 paid to Alpha Ltd was correctly recorded in John Smith's ledger but was not shown on the statement from Alpha Ltd.

The balance on the statement from Alpha Ltd. was:

    A   £748

    B   £1,248

    C   £1,788

    D   £2,288

Section 30

Control Accounts

If you have difficulty with any of the questions in this section, you should refer to Chapter 30 of **Frank Wood's Business Accounting 1** *(Seventh edition)*

30.1 The total amount of money received from debtors, in addition to being recorded in the bank account, should be . . .

    A   credited to the sales account.

    B   credited to the debtors control account.

    C   debited to the debtors control account.

    D   debited to the sales account.

30.2 In a sales ledger control account, bad debts written off should be shown as . . .

    A   a debit.

    B   a balance carried down.

    C   a credit.

    D   both a debit and a credit.

30.3 The balance on a firm's debtors control account at the end of a year should agree with . . .

    A   the total of the firm's sales for that year.

    B   the amount of money received from debtors during the year.

    C   the total of debtors which are outstanding for more than one year.

    D   the total of its list of debtors outstanding at the year-end.

30.4 The balance on a firm's creditors control account at the end of an accounting period should equal . . .

    A   the total amount which the firm paid to its creditors during the period.

    B   the firm's total purchases for the period.

    C   the total of its list of creditors outstanding at the end of the period.

    D   the cost of the firm's sales for the period.

30.5 A credit balance brought down on a debtors control account *cannot* be explained by . . .

    A   a credit note issued to a debtor immediately after he had paid his account in full.

    B   a debtor paying more than the amount owed by him.

    C   unrecorded returns outwards.

    D   discount allowed recorded twice in the debtors control account.

30.6 Over the course of an accounting period, the amount owed to a firm by its debtors increased by £50,000. During the period, credit sales totalled £230,000 and money received from debtors amounted to £190,000. The £10,000 apparent discrepancy could be due to unrecorded . . .

    A   discount allowed.

    B   bad debts.

    C   sales returns.

    D   credit sales.

30.7 At the beginning of an accounting period a firm owed its creditors £15,000. During the period, the firm's credit purchases amounted to £87,000 and it paid £94,000 to its creditors.

Assuming there were no other transactions relating to creditors, at the end of the accounting period the firm owed its creditors . . .

    A   £7,000

    B   £8,000

    C   £14,000

    D   £22,000

30.8 At the beginning of an accounting period, a firm was owed £900 by its debtors. At the end of the same accounting period the firm's debtors owed £1,500. During the period, a bad debt of £100 was written off and £5,000 was received from credit customers.

The total of the firm's credit sales for the period was:

    A   £3,700

    B   £4,200

    C   £5,700

    D   £5,900

30.9 Over the course of an accounting period the amount owed by a firm to its creditors decreased by £20,000. During the period the firm's purchases totalled £950,000, of which 80% were on credit. The firm did not receive any discount from its suppliers during the period. On the basis of the foregoing information, the amount which the firm paid to its creditors during the period was:

    A   £740,000

    B   £760,000

    C   £780,000

    D   £930,000

30.10 Given the following information, calculate the amount owed to a firm by its debtors at 31 December.

Debtors at 1 January	£ 11,500
Credit sales for the period 1 January - 31 December	48,000
Money received from debtors between 1 January and 31 December	45,000

    A   £8,500

    B   £14,500

    C   £18,500

    D   £83,500

30.11 A firm's creditors at the beginning of an accounting period totalled £2,500 and at the end of the same accounting period they totalled £4,200. If the firm paid £32,000 to its creditors during the period, its credit purchases for the period totalled:

    A   £30,300

    B   £31,600

    C   £33,700

    D   None of the above.

30.12 Given the following information, what is the balance on the creditors control account at 31 December ?

Credit balance on the creditors control account at 1 January	£ 4,600
Transactions for the period 1 January to 31 December	
Discount received	1,000
Credit purchases	54,000
Credit purchases returns	6,000
Refunds received from suppliers	2,000
Payments to suppliers	39,000
Balance in creditors ledger set off against debtors ledger	1,000

    A   £8,600

    B   £9,600

    C   £12,600

    D   £13,600

30.13 Before considering bad debts, the balance on a firm's debtors control account is £1,000 (debit) and the balance on its provision for bad debts account is £25 (credit). Subsequently, a bad debt of £50 is written off. The balance on the debtors control account in the nominal (general) ledger after writing off the above bad debt is . . .

    A   £925

    B   £950

    C   £975

    D   £1,000

30.14 The balance on a firm's debtors control account is £6,000, the balance on its bad debts account is £300 and the balance on its provision for bad debts account is £285.

If a bad debt of £300, previously written off, is subsequently recovered, the correct balance on the debtors control account in the nominal (general) ledger, after recording the recovery, is:

    A   £5,415

    B   £5,700

    C   £6,000

    D   None of the above.

30.15 The following information relates to a firm whose policy is to maintain a provision for bad and doubtful debts equal to 5% of its debtors.

Balances at 1 January	
Debtors	£ 10,000
Provision for bad and doubtful debts	500
Transactions for the period 1 January to 31 December	
Credit sales	30,000
Cash sales	5,000
Receipts from credit customers	25,000
Bad debts written off	1,000

The balance on the firm's debtors control account at 31 December is:

    A   £13,300

    B   £14,000

    C   £14,250

    D   £15,000

30.16 The following information relates to a firm's most recent accounting period.

Debtors at 1 January	£ 8,000
Transactions for the period 1 January to 31 December	
Discount allowed	1,000
Credit sales	89,000
Receipts from debtors	80,000
Cash sales	6,000
Returns inwards	6,000

The balance on the firm's debtors control account at 31 December was:

- A £3,000
- B £10,000
- C £11,000
- D £17,000

30.17 The following information relates to a firm's most recent accounting period.

Creditors at 1 January	£ 5,000
Transactions for the period 1 January to 31 December	
Discount received	500
Credit purchases	60,000
Payments to suppliers	54,000
Cash purchases	7,000
Returns outwards	3,500

The balance on the firm's creditors control account at 31 December was:

- A £1,000
- B £7,000
- C £8,000
- D £13,000

30.18 At the start of a financial year a firm's gross debtors amounted to £5,000. At the end of the year this amount had increased by 20%. During the year £15,000 was received from debtors and discounts totalling £1,000 were allowed to debtors. Bad debts written off amounted to £2,000 and £4,000 was received from a debtor previously written off as bad. Credit sales for the year were:

- A £14,000
- B £15,000
- C £19,000
- D £20,000

30.19 A firm which sells exclusively on credit allows a discount of 2% to its customers if they pay by the due date, which they always do. The following details are available for the firm's most recent financial year:

Amount owed by debtors at the beginning of the year	£ 22,000
Amount owed by debtors at the end of the year	24,000
Bad debts written off during the year	3,500
Money received from debtors during the year	147,000

The firm's credit sales for the year were:

    A   £148,469

    B   £152,500

    C   £155,500

    D   £155,612

30.20 A firm listed its debtors balances. These totalled £29,175. The balance on the firm's sales ledger control account did not agree with this total. Upon investigation, the following errors were discovered.

- A credit balance of £80 on one debtor's account in the sales ledger had been listed as a debit balance.
- A debit balance of £67 on another debtor's account in the sales ledger had been listed as a credit balance.
- £220 received from a debtor had been entered in the purchases ledger instead of the sales ledger.
- The list of balances had been overcast by £72.

The correct (debit) balance on the sales ledger control account is:

    A   £28,857

    B   £28,870

    C   £29,001

    D   £29,297

30.21 A firm's list of debtors' balances, which totalled £39,150, did not agree with its debtors ledger control account. Upon investigation, the following errors were discovered.

- A credit balance of £70 on one debtor's account in the sales ledger had been listed as a debit balance.
- A debit balance of £40 on another debtor's account in the sales ledger had been listed as a credit balance.
- The list of balances had been overcast by £60.

The correct debit balance brought down on the debtors ledger control account is:

    A   £39,030

    B   £39,060

    C   £39,150

    D   £39,210

30.22 The balance of £37,564 in a firm's purchases ledger control account did not agree with the total of the creditors' balances listed at the same date. Upon investigation, the following errors were discovered:

- A refund of £140 received from a credit supplier because of an overpayment had been posted to the wrong side of the control account.
- Returns outwards of £310 had also been posted to the wrong side of the control account.
- The list of balances had been undercast by £200.
- Discounts received of £276 were not recorded in the control account.

The correct credit balance on the purchases ledger control account is:

    A   £36,948

    B   £37,118

    C   £37,500

    D   £37,628

30.23 Which of the following errors, on its own, could account for the total of the balances in a firm's debtors ledger being £800 more than the debit balance on its debtors control account?

    A   Discounts allowed totalling £800 have been omitted from the nominal (general) ledger but correctly accounted for in the debtors' ledger.

    B   One debtors' ledger account with a credit balance of £800 has been treated as a debit balance when totalling the balances in the debtors' ledger.

    C   The total amount received from debtors, as shown in the cash book (or cash receipts book) is overstated by £800.

    D   None of the above.

Section 31

Errors not Affecting Trial Balance Agreement

If you have difficulty with any of the questions in this section, you should refer to Chapter 31 of **Frank Wood's Business Accounting 1** *(Seventh edition)*

31.1 Which of the following is an error of principle ?

    A   A sales invoice for an incorrect amount was correctly entered in the sales journal.

    B   Stock was issued but an accompanying invoice was not.

    C   The wrong percentage rate was used when calculating depreciation.

    D   An item was entered in the wrong class of account.

31.2 If the cost of servicing a firm's car was debited to a fixed asset account instead of being debited to the motor expenses account . . .

    A   gross profit would be overstated.

    B   net profit would be understated.

    C   expenses would be understated.

    D   net assets would be understated.

31.3 The journal is used to correct errors because . . .

    A   it is faster to record the corrections in the Journal than in the ledger.

    B   once entered in the Journal, there is no need to record the corrections in the ledger.

    C   a narrative can be included in the Journal to explain the nature of the transaction and therefore explain the entries in the double-entry records.

    D   it is easier to correct errors using the Journal than to correct them in the control accounts.

Section 32

Suspense Accounts and Errors

If you have difficulty with any of the questions in this section, you should refer to Chapter 32 of **Frank Wood's Business Accounting 1** *(Seventh edition)*

32.1 Which of the following errors would be disclosed by a trial balance?

    A   Expenses being debited to the sales account.

    B   A credit sale of £300 inadvertently entered in the Sales Journal as £30.

    C   Failure to record a cash purchase.

    D   None of the above.

32.2 If a trial balance does not balance, which of the following accounts should be opened?

    A   A suspense account.

    B   A control account.

    C   A provision account.

    D   A liability account.

32.3 Which of the following should be entered in a suspense account?

    A   Miscellaneous expenses.

    B   Any difference between the debit and credit totals of the trial balance which cannot be immediately located pending further investigation.

    C   Bad debts recovered.

    D   None of the above.

32.4 If there is a material (significant) debit balance on a suspense account . . .

    A   it should be included as an asset in the balance sheet.

    B   it should be included as an expense in the profit and loss account.

    C   it should be included as a liability in the balance sheet.

    D   the underlying error(s) should be located and corrected before preparing financial statements.

32.5 Bank charges should initially be recorded . . .

    A   by debiting the bank charges account and crediting the bank account.

    B   by debiting the bank account and crediting the bank charges account.

    C   in the Cash Book (or Cheque Payments Book).

    D   by debiting the suspense account and crediting the bank account.

Section 33

Introduction to Accounting Ratios

*If you have difficulty with any of the questions in this section, you should refer to Chapter 33 of **Frank Wood's Business Accounting 1** (Seventh edition)*

33.1 The gross profit margin earned on an item which cost £500 and is sold for £625 is:

    A   20%

    B   25%

    C   33 1/3%

    D   None of the above.

33.2 The mark-up on an item which cost £500 and is sold for £625 is:

    A   20%

    B   25%

    C   33 1/3%

    D   None of the above.

33.3 The gross profit margin earned by a shopkeeper who sells all goods at 25% above their cost is:

    A   20%

    B   30%

    C   33 1/3 %

    D   35%

33.4 A firm's gross profit margin is 20%. Its mark-up on cost is:

    A   16 2/3rds %

    B   22%

    C   25%

    D   30%

33.5 A firm's cost of sales for a particular accounting period was £16,000. During the period, it earned a gross profit margin of 20% on all goods sold. The firm's sales for the accounting period were:

    A   £13,600

    B   £20,160

    C   £21,000

    D   None of the above.

33.6 The following information relates to a retail business whose financial year ends on 31 December.

Sales for the period 1 January - 31 December	£ 240,000
Stock at 1 January	10,300
Purchases for the period 1 January - 31 December	186,000
Percentage mark-up applied during the period 1 January - 31 December	33 1/3%

The firm's stock at 31 December, at cost, was:

    A   £4,300

    B   £16,300

    C   £36,300

    D   None of the above.

33.7 The following information relates to a sole trader whose financial year ends on 31 December.

Sales for the period 1 January - 31 December	£ 200,000
Purchases for the period 1 January - 31 December	130,000
Stock at 1 January	50,000
Percentage mark-up applied on all goods during the period 1 January - 31 December	25%

The sole trader's stock at 31 December, at cost, was:

    A   £20,000

    B   £26,000

    C   £40,000

    D   £70,000

33.8 A business' rate of stock turnover during any given accounting period is calculated as . . .

    A   the business' sales for that period divided by the value of its stock at the beginning of the period.

    B   the business' sales for that period divided by the value of its stock at the end of the period.

    C   the business' purchases for that period divided by the value of its stock at the end of the period.

    D   the business' cost of sales for that period divided by the average of the business' stock during the period (the average being the sum of its stock at the beginning of the period and its stock at the end of the period divided by two).

Section 34

Single Entry and Incomplete Records

If you have difficulty with any of the questions in this section, you should refer to Chapter 34 of **Frank Wood's Business Accounting 1** *(Seventh edition)*

34.1 Over the course of an accounting period a business' debtors increased by £40,000. If 80% of the business' total sales of £750,000 were made on credit, no discount was allowed to debtors and no bad debts were written off, the amount of money received from debtors during the period was:

    A   £560,000

    B   £640,000

    C   £710,000

    D   £790,000

34.2 At the end of its most recent financial year, a firm, which sells exclusively on credit, was owed £60,000 by its debtors. The firm applies a mark-up of 25% on all goods and allows its debtors 60 days' credit (based on 360 days in the firm's financial year). Its gross profit for the year was:

    A   £72,000

    B   £90,000

    C   £122,000

    D   £180,000

34.3 Catherine O'Byrne's trade is seasonal. Her monthly sales are 50% higher in the three summer months than in the other nine months of the year. She earns a gross margin of 25% in the summer months and 20% during the rest of the year. If her total sales for the year ended 30 April were £283,500, her cost of sales for the same period was:

    A   £212,625

    B   £222,075

    C   £223,256

    D   £226,800

34.4 A firm has net assets of £8,000, net current assets of £3,000 and no long-term debt. Its fixed assets are:

    A   £3,000

    B   £5,000

    C   £8,000

    D   The total of fixed assets cannot be ascertained from the information provided.

34.5 A firm's capital at the beginning of a year was £16,500 and its capital at the end of the same year was £11,350. The proprietor's drawings during the year totalled £3,300 and no new capital was introduced. The firm's profit or loss for the year was:

  A   Loss of £1,850

  B   Profit of £1,850

  C   Loss of £8,450

  D   Profit of £8,450

34.6 The following information relates to a hardware merchant, who is not registered for VAT and who makes all purchases on credit.

	at 31 December 1996	at 31 December 1995
Stock	£ 10,600	£ 10,300
Debtors	5,400	4,800
Creditors	5,900	6,300
Transactions during 1996		
Amount received from debtors		£ 127,600
Amount paid to creditors		93,200
Cash sales		23,200
Discount allowed to debtors		2,400
Bad debts written off		800
Increase in provision for doubtful debts		250
Refunds received from creditors		80

The gross profit earned by the merchant during 1996 was:

  A   £38,820

  B   £38,870

  C   £61,750

  D   £62,180

Section 35

Receipts & Payments Accounts and Income & Expenditure Accounts

*If you have difficulty with any of the questions in this section, you should refer to Chapter 35 of **Frank Wood's Business Accounting 1** (Seventh edition)*

35.1 A Receipts and Payments Account is . . .

    A   a summary of revenues and expenses for a period.

    B   a summary of cash and bank transactions for a period.

    C   a summary of purchases and sales for a period.

    D   None of the above.

35.2 The balancing figure in an entity's Receipts and Payments Account for an accounting period is . . .

    A   the net profit earned or loss incurred by the entity for the period.

    B   the sum of its cash and bank balances at the end of the period.

    C   the excess of its income over its expenditure for the period.

    D   the excess of its expenditure over its income for the period.

35.3 If a club operates a bar at a profit, this profit should be accounted for in the club's income and expenditure account by . . .

    A   including sales and expenses relating to the bar separately.

    B   including it in the income section of the account.

    C   including receipts and payments relating to the bar separately.

    D   including any surplus of receipts over payments in the account.

35.4 A club's accumulated fund is . . .

    A   the amount (if any) by which its assets exceed its liabilities.

    B   the amount of its liabilities.

    C   the aggregate depreciation on its fixed assets.

    D   the same as its bank balance.

35.5 In the accounts of a club, which of the following is an asset ?

    A   Subscriptions receivable by the club.

    B   Subscriptions received in advance by the club.

    C   Subscriptions received by the club.

    D   None of the above.

35.6 A club which has fifty members charges an annual membership subscription of £20. At the beginning of the year, five members had paid their subscription in advance and four were in arrears with their subscriptions. At the end of the year, three members were in arrears with their subscription and two members had paid the following year's subscription. The club's subscription income for the year was:

    A   £960

    B   £1,000

    C   £1,020

    D   £1,040

35.7 A club which has fifty members charges an annual membership subscription of £20. At the beginning of the year, five members had paid their subscription in advance and four were in arrears with their subscriptions. At the end of the year, three members were in arrears with their subscription and two members had paid the following year's subscription. The amount received by the club during the year in respect of subscriptions was:

    A   £960

    B   £1,000

    C   £1,020

    D   £1,040

35.8 If some members of a club have not paid their annual subscription by the end of the club's financial year and the club decides not to include the subscriptions due as revenue for the year, the club is applying . . .

    A   the consistency concept.

    B   the going concern concept.

    C   the prudence concept.

    D   the entity concept.

35.9 A credit balance brought down on a club's life subscriptions account represents . . .

    A   a long-term loan to life members.

    B   life subscriptions received by the club but not yet credited in its income and expenditure account.

    C   subscriptions due from life members.

    D   revenue for the current year.

Section 36

Manufacturing Accounts

*If you have difficulty with any of the questions in this section, you should refer to Chapter 36 of **Frank Wood's Business Accounting 1** (Seventh edition)*

36.1 Each of the following items should appear in either a manufacturing account or a profit and loss account. Categorise each item as either 'M' if it should appear in the manufacturing account or 'P&L' if it should appear in the profit and loss account and choose the option A, B, C or D which correctly categorises all three items.

Item 1	Depreciation of productive plant and machinery for the current accounting period.
Item 2	A factory supervisor's wages.
Item 3	Depreciation of an office building for the current accounting period.

	Item 1	Item 2	Item 3
A	M	M	P&L
B	M	P&L	M
C	M	M	M
D	P&L	M	P&L

36.2 Which of the following should be charged as an expense in the profit and loss account of a manufacturing firm?

- A   Office rent.
- B   Work in progress.
- C   Direct material costs.
- D   Carriage charged on raw materials purchased.

36.3 Which of the following is calculated in a manufacturing account?

- A   The total production costs paid during an accounting period.
- B   The total cost of goods produced during an accounting period.
- C   The production cost of goods completed during an accounting period.
- D   The gross profit on goods sold during an accounting period.

36.4 In the accounts of a manufacturing firm, 'production cost' equals . . .

    A   the cost of direct materials acquired.

    B   the sum of direct material costs and direct wages.

    C   the sum of direct expenses, direct material costs, direct wages and production overheads.

    D   the sum of direct expenses, direct material costs, direct wages, production overheads and administration expenses.

36.5 When preparing a manufacturing account, a distinction is made between direct costs and indirect costs. Categorise each of the following items as either direct or indirect costs and choose the option A, B, C or D which correctly categorises all four items.

Item 1	Royalties payable relating to the production process in use.
Item 2	The cost of acquiring raw materials.
Item 3	Wages paid to production line operators in respect of the current accounting period.
Item 4	Wages of a production supervisor.

	Item 1	Item 2	Item 3	Item 4
A	Direct	Direct	Direct	Direct
B	Indirect	Direct	Direct	Direct
C	Indirect	Direct	Direct	Indirect
D	Direct	Direct	Direct	Indirect

36.6 Which of the following is a direct cost for a firm which manufactures and sells Grecian urns ?

    A   A royalty charge based on the number of urns produced.

    B   The cost of lubricating oils for machinery and vehicles.

    C   The factory supervisor's salary.

    D   None of the above.

36.7 Which of the following costs would *not* normally be included in the calculation of 'cost of sales' in the profit and loss account of a manufacturing firm ?

    A   Depreciation on the factory premises.

    B   Bad debts written off.

    C   Carriage charged on raw materials purchased.

    D   None of the above.

36.8 'Prime cost' does *not* include . . .

    A   direct labour costs.

    B   factory overhead expenses.

    C   the cost of raw materials consumed.

    D   direct expenses.

36.9 Which of the following costs should be included in the calculation of 'prime cost' in a manufacturing account ?

    A   The cost, incurred by the firm for which the manufacturing account is being prepared, of transporting raw materials from a supplier's premises.

    B   The wages of factory workers wholly engaged in machine maintenance.

    C   The depreciation of lorries used for deliveries to customers.

    D   The cost of indirect production materials.

36.10 In the accounts of a manufacturing firm, the cost of direct labour . . .

    A   should be included as part of the prime cost.

    B   should be included in factory overheads.

    C   should be included in the Profit and Loss Account.

    D   should be divided between the prime cost and the cost of factory overheads.

36.11 In the accounts of a manufacturing firm, depreciation of factory plant and equipment should be included under the heading of . . .

    A   direct expenses.

    B   cost of raw materials consumed.

    C   administrative expenses.

    D   factory overheads.

36.12 In the accounts of a manufacturing firm, accountancy fees in respect of the current accounting period should be included under the heading . . .

    A   prime cost.

    B   selling and distribution expenses.

    C   factory overheads.

    D   administrative expenses.

36.13 In the accounts of a manufacturing firm, the cost of raw materials used during an accounting period should be included under the heading . . .

    A   factory overhead expenses.

    B   administrative expenses.

    C   prime cost.

    D   selling and distribution expenses.

36.14 The following costs were incurred by a manufacturer of cut glass during 1996.

Raw material costs	£ 250,000
Labour costs	
Glass blowers	100,000
Maintenance staff	10,000
Administration staff	20,000
Cost of hiring equipment used in crystal production	12,000
Heating and lighting costs	21,000

The prime cost for the year was:

    A   £350,000

    B   £362,000

    C   £372,000

    D   £413,000

36.15 The following information relates to a manufacturing firm.

	at 1 January	at 31 December
Stock of finished goods	£ 2,000	£ 1,500
Stock of raw materials	750	500
For the period . . .		
Distribution expenses		485
Discount allowed		980
Purchase of raw materials		1,750
Salaries of sales staff		1,200
Carriage inwards		500
Indirect production costs		6,200
Sales		20,250
Direct labour		1,000

The firm's gross profit for the year was:

    A   £8,850

    B   £9,565

    C   £10,050

    D   £10,550

36.16 Which of the following methods of providing for depreciation produces a charge which is lowest in the first year of an asset's life and rises thereafter ?

    A   Reducing balance.

    B   Sum-of-the-years'-digits.

    C   Straight-line.

    D   None of the above.

Section 37

Departmental Accounts

If you have difficulty with any of the questions in this section, you should refer to Chapter 37 of **Frank Wood's Business Accounting 1** *(Seventh edition)*

37.1 The purpose of preparing a departmental profit and loss account for a firm is . . .

    A   to show the relative financial performance of different sections of the firm.

    B   to estimate the firm's future cash requirements.

    C   to ensure that all likely bad debts are provided for.

    D   to ensure that discounts allowed by the firm do not exceed discounts received by it.

37.2 When preparing a departmental trading and profit and loss account, the best method of allocating expenses between departments is . . .

    A   to allocate expenses to each department in proportion to the sales of that department.

    B   to charge against each department those costs which are within its control.

    C   to allocate expenses to each department in proportion to the purchases of that department.

    D   None of the above.

Section 38

Partnership Accounts: An Introduction

If you have difficulty with any of the questions in this section, you should refer to Chapter 38 of **Frank Wood's Business Accounting 1** *(Seventh edition).*

38.1 A partnership . . .

    A   must be formed by deed.

    B   must be formed by agreement in writing.

    C   may be formed by verbal agreement.

    D   None of the above.

38.2 The rights and liabilities of partners among themselves . . .

    A   may be freely agreed.

    B   must be agreed with the partnership's creditors.

    C   are governed by the Partnership Act, 1890.

    D   None of the above.

38.3 The minimum number of general partners which a limited partnership must have is:

    A   1

    B   2

    C   3

    D   7

38.4 In order for partners' capitals to remain fixed, their respective shares of profits must be . . .

    A   debited to their capital accounts.

    B   credited to their capital accounts.

    C   debited to their current accounts.

    D   credited to their current accounts.

38.5 In the absence of a partnership agreement, the Partnership Act, 1890, among other things, requires that . . .

    A   partners share profits equally and interest on capital is paid at the rate of 5% per annum.

    B   partners share profits in relation to the balances on their capital accounts and interest on capital is paid at the rate of 5% per annum.

    C   partners share profits equally and interest on capital is not paid.

    D   partners share profits in relation to the balances on their capital accounts and interest on capital is not paid.

38.6 John and Mary, the only two partners in a firm, invested capital of £40,000 and £60,000 respectively and agreed their entitlements to be:

	John	*Mary*
Annual salary	£14,000	£20,000
Interest on capital (per annum)	10%	10%
Share of remaining profit or loss	40%	60%

If the profit for the year was £80,000, how much, in total, would John be entitled to receive ?

    A   £14,400

    B   £18,000

    C   £21,600

    D   £32,400

38.7 Jack and Diane, the only two partners in a firm, invested capital of £20,000 and £30,000 respectively and agreed their entitlements to be:

	Jack	*Diane*
Annual salary	£18,000	£22,000
Interest on capital (per annum)	10%	10%
Share of remaining profit or loss	40%	60%

If the profit for the year was £40,000, what share would be debited / credited to Diane's current account ?

    A   Nil

    B   £3,000 Debit

    C   £22,000 Credit

    D   £24,000 Credit

38.8 Tom and Joan formed a partnership. In addition to investing £15,000, Tom transferred ownership of a building, which had cost him £45,000, to the partnership. At the time of the transfer, the market value of the building was £60,000. The mortgage of £35,000 on the building was taken over by the partnership. The amount to be recorded in Tom's capital account is:

    A   £25,000

    B   £40,000

    C   £60,000

    D   £75,000

Section 39

Goodwill in Partnership Accounts

If you have difficulty with any of the questions in this section, you should refer to Chapter 39 of **Frank Wood's Business Accounting 1** *(Seventh edition)*

39.1 Joe is buying a firm whose only assets are valued as follows. Buildings £50,000, Vehicles £15,000, Fixtures £5,000 and Stock £40,000. The firm does not have any liabilities. He is to pay £140,000 for the firm. This means that:

    A   He is paying £40,000 for goodwill.

    B   The buildings he is acquiring are costing him £30,000 more than they are worth.

    C   He is paying £30,000 for goodwill.

    D   He has made an arithmetical mistake.

39.2 John earns an annual net income of £19,500 from a photography business which he runs. He has capital of £35,000 invested in this business. If he ceased running his own business and worked as an employee in another photographic business he would earn a salary of £11,000 per annum. If he could invest his capital elsewhere in a project with the same degree of risk as his own business he could expect a return of 6.5% per annum. If goodwill in this type of firm is valued at five years' purchase of super-profits, the goodwill of John's business is:

    A   £31,125

    B   £37,500

    C   £40,225

    D   £42,500

39.3 Albert, Ben and Catherine are in partnership sharing profits and losses in the ratio Albert 1/2 : Ben 1/3rd : Catherine 1/6th. On 31 December Albert retired from the partnership and Dymphna was admitted, the new profit sharing ratio being Ben 2/7ths : Catherine 4/7ths : Dymphna 1/7th. For the purposes of these changes, goodwill, which is not to be included in the accounts, is calculated at three times the current year's net profit of £10,500. The net adjustment on Ben's capital account in respect of goodwill is:

    A   a net credit of £1,500.

    B   a net debit of £7,500.

    C   a net debit of £12,750.

    D   no adjustment.

Section 40

Partnership Accounts Continued: The Revaluation of Assets

If you have difficulty with any of the questions in this section, you should refer to Chapter 40 of **Frank Wood's Business Accounting 1** *(Seventh edition)*

40.1 Frequently, when there is a change of partners in a partnership, assets are revalued because . . .

    A   this is a requirement of the Partnership Act, 1890.

    B   it helps prevent financial injustice to some partners.

    C   inflation affects all values.

    D   None of the above.

40.2 If a partnership revalues its assets upon the retirement of one of the partners, any resulting loss should be . . .

    A   credited to the old partners' capital accounts in the old profit sharing ratios.

    B   credited to the new partners' capital accounts in the new profit sharing ratios.

    C   debited to the old partners' capital accounts in the old profit sharing ratios.

    D   debited to the new partners' capital accounts in the new profit sharing ratios.

Section 41

An Introduction to the Final Accounts of Limited Liability Companies

If you have difficulty with any of the questions in this section, you should refer to Chapter 41 of **Frank Wood's Business Accounting 1** *(Seventh edition)*

41.1 One disadvantage of a limited company, relative to other forms of business organisation, is . . .

    A   greater regulation.

    B   the fact that the company's liability is limited.

    C   the fact that the company is a legal entity separate and distinct from its owner(s).

    D   None of the above.

41.2 A person who acquires shares in a company is known as . . .

    A   a shareholder.

    B   a director.

    C   a partner.

    D   None of the above.

41.3 In a limited company . . .

    A   the liability of the shareholders is limited.

    B   the liability of the company is limited.

    C   the liability of both the shareholders and the company is limited.

    D   None of the above.

41.4 The liability of a shareholder in a limited company, to the company, cannot exceed . . .

    A   any amount unpaid on his / her shares.

    B   the amount called up on his / her shares.

    C   the total value of his / her personal net assets.

    D   None of the above.

41.5 A PLC is . . .

    A   a company whose shares are 'listed' on a recognised Stock Exchange.

    B   a public limited company.

    C   a private limited company.

    D   a public sector body.

41.6 A public limited company registered in the United Kingdom must have an authorised share capital of at least . . .

    A   £7,500.

    B   £30,000.

    C   £50,000.

    D   None of the above.

41.7 The right to transfer shares in a private company . . .

    A   may be restricted.

    B   must be restricted.

    C   cannot be restricted.

    D   None of the above.

41.8 A company's authorised share capital is . . .

    A   the amount of share capital the company has issued.

    B   the amount of share capital which the directors of the company intend to issue.

    C   the amount of share capital stated in the company's original Memorandum of Association.

    D   the maximum amount of share capital which the company currently has the power to issue.

41.9 The amount of the issued share capital of a company is . . .

    A   always equal to the amount of its authorised share capital.

    B   equal to the amount of its issued preference share capital.

    C   equal to the reserves of the company.

    D   None of the above.

41.10 A dividend is . . .

    A   a share of a company's profit.

    B   interest paid on a company's borrowings.

    C   always paid to banks and other creditors.

    D   None of the above.

41.11 A company has declared a final dividend for the year ended 31 March and proposes to pay it on 10 May. Which of the following is the correct treatment of this item in the financial statements for the year ended 31 March ?

    A   Show the amount of the dividend as an expense in the profit and loss account and as a current liability in the balance sheet.

    B   Show the amount of the dividend as a deduction in the profit and loss appropriation account and as a current liability in the balance sheet.

    C   Show the amount of the dividend as a deduction in the profit and loss appropriation account and reduce the bank balance shown in the balance sheet accordingly.

    D   None of the above.

41.12 The declaration of a dividend by a company . . .

    A   reduces the company's bank balance.

    B   increases the company's liabilities.

    C   increases the shareholders' funds in the company.

    D   does not affect the shareholders' funds in the company.

41.13 A company issued 20,000 25p ordinary shares at a premium of 20%. The market value of these shares is currently 40p per share. As a result of this issue, share capital, as shown in the balance sheet, will be increased by:

    A   £4,000

    B   £5,000

    C   £6,000

    D   £8,000

41.14 Shareholders' funds in a company equals . . .

    A   the total of share capital, reserves and long-term debts of the company.

    B   the total of share capital and revenue reserves of the company.

    C   the total of issued share capital and reserves of the company.

    D   the total of share capital and capital reserves of the company.

41.15 If a company makes a transfer from its profit and loss account to a capital reserve . . .

    A   shareholders' funds will be increased.

    B   the relevant amount of money will be transferred to a special bank account.

    C   shareholders' funds will be decreased.

    D   shareholders' funds will remain unchanged.

41.16 A company wishes to pay the maximum possible ordinary dividend in respect of a year during which it earned a net profit, after tax, of £26,600. The company has issued 20,000 £1 8% preference shares and 50,000 £1 ordinary shares. If £5,000 is to be transferred to the general reserve, what ordinary dividends are to be paid, in percentage terms?

    A   10%

    B   20%

    C   40%

    D   60%

41.17 A company has the following capital structure:

	Authorised	Issued
25p 4% Preference shares	£ 400,000	£ 100,000
£2 Ordinary shares	£ 500,000	£ 200,000

If the company declares a dividend of 10p per ordinary share, the total dividend payable by the company will be:

    A   £14,000

    B   £26,000

    C   £54,000

    D   £66,000

41.18 A limited company's revenue reserves increased from £15,000 at 1 January to £31,000 at 31 December. If the company earned a profit for the year of £27,000, after tax, dividends for the year were:

    A   £4,000

    B   £11,000

    C   £12,000

    D   £45,000

41.19 The authorised share capital of a company is comprised of £150,000 of 50p ordinary shares and 50,000 6% preference shares of £1 each. Ordinary shares with a nominal (par) value of £100,000 and all of the preference shares have been issued and are fully paid. If the company pays the preference dividend and proposes to pay an ordinary dividend of 10p per share, then the total dividends payable by the company will be:

    A   £13,000

    B   £18,000

    C   £23,000

    D   £33,000

41.20 The balance on the profit and loss account, as shown in the balance sheet of a company, represents:

    A   any profit earned by the company during the most recent accounting period.

    B   the cumulative profits earned by the company since the date of its incorporation, less any losses, dividends, or transfers to reserves.

    C   money set aside for specific future uses.

    D   money available for daily operations.

41.21 In the balance sheet of a limited company, the profit and loss account balance is shown under the heading . . .

    A   'current liabilities'.

    B   'fixed assets'.

    C   'current assets'.

    D   'capital and reserves'.

41.22 Which of the following is *not* normally found in the capital and reserves section of a company's balance sheet?

    A   Share premium account.

    B   Profit and loss account balance.

    C   Dividends payable.

    D   Ordinary share capital.

41.23 In the accounts of a limited company, remuneration paid to directors, during the current accounting period, in respect of the same period . . .

    A   is shown as an appropriation of profit.

    B   is shown as part of the company's cost of sales.

    C   is shown as an expense in the profit and loss account.

    D   None of the above.

41.24 In the accounts of a limited company, the balance on a provision for depreciation account . . .

    A   is shown under the heading 'current liabilities'.

    B   is shown under the heading 'capital and reserves'.

    C   is shown as an appropriation of profit.

    D   is deducted from the cost or valuation of the related fixed assets.

41.25 In the accounts of a limited company, debenture interest paid during the current accounting period, in respect of the same period . . .

    A   is part of the company's cost of sales.

    B   is an expense.

    C   is an appropriation of profit.

    D   None of the above.

41.26 Which of the following should be shown in the profit and loss appropriation account of a limited company ?

    A   Debenture interest paid during the current accounting period, in respect of the same period.

    B   Dividends paid during the current accounting period, in respect of the same period.

    C   Directors' remuneration paid during the current accounting period, in respect of the same period.

    D   None of the above.

41.27 Which of the following cannot normally be determined from the financial statements of a public limited company whose shares are quoted on the Stock Exchange ?

    A   The nominal (par) value of the issued ordinary share capital of the company.

    B   The book value of the company's fixed assets.

    C   The current market value of the issued ordinary share capital of the company.

    D   None of the above.

41.28 The total of the net assets of a company is equal to . . .

    A   The nominal (par) value of the company's share capital.

    B   The market value of the company's share capital.

    C   The amount paid by shareholders for their shares.

    D   The book value of the shareholders' interest in the company.

41.29 In the case of a company which has issued both cumulative preference shares and ordinary shares, which of the following statements is true ?

    A   If the dividend on the cumulative preference shares is not paid when due, an ordinary dividend cannot be paid until all arrears of the preference dividend have first been paid.

    B   If the dividend on the cumulative preference shares for the current year is not paid when due, the company may pay an ordinary dividend next year once next year's preference dividend is paid first.

    C   A dividend must be paid on the ordinary shares before any dividend can be paid on the cumulative preference shares.

    D   None of the above.

41.30 A company issued ordinary shares at their nominal (par) value and received payment in full. The effect of this on the company's financial statements is . . .

    A   the bank balance is increased and the figure shown in the balance sheet for ordinary share capital is increased.

    B   the bank balance is decreased and the figure shown in the balance sheet for ordinary share capital is decreased.

    C   the bank balance is increased and the figure shown in the balance sheet for ordinary share capital is decreased.

    D   None of the above.

41.31 In the accounts of a company, goodwill (when it exists) . . .

    A   must be a debit balance.

    B   must be a credit balance.

    C   can be either a debit or a credit balance.

    D   cannot exist.

41.32 Goodwill may arise in a company's financial statements if . . .

    A   the company acquires another company for more than the fair value of its separable net assets.

    B   the company sells a fixed asset at a profit.

    C   the market value of its shares exceeds their nominal (par) value.

    D   None of the above.

41.33 In the financial statements of a company, goodwill should be shown . . .

    A   under the heading 'current assets'.

    B   under the heading 'intangible fixed assets'.

    C   under the heading 'tangible fixed assets'.

    D   None of the above.

41.34 Financial Reporting Standards are issued by . . .

    A   the Stock Exchange.

    B   the government.

    C   the Accounting Standards Board.

    D   None of the above.

41.35 The abbreviation 'SSAP' means . . .

    A   Statement of Standard Accounting Principles.

    B   Statutory Statement of Accounting Principles.

    C   Statement of Standard Accounting Practice.

    D   None of the above.

41.36 Statements of Standard Accounting Practice and Financial Reporting Standards should be applied when preparing the financial statements . . .

    A   of any entity whose accounts are intended to give a true and fair view of its financial position and its profit or loss.

    B   of private companies only.

    C   of public limited companies (PLCs) only.

    D   of companies whose shares are listed on a recognised Stock Exchange only.

41.37 Prior to issuing a Financial Reporting Standard, the Accounting Standards Board normally issues a 'draft' with a view to obtaining comments on the proposed Standard. Such a 'draft' document is referred to as . . .

    A   an Exposure Draft.

    B   an Example Draft.

    C   an Explanation Draft.

    D   a Financial Reporting Exposure Draft (FRED).

41.38 The format in which the financial statements of UK registered limited companies must be published is prescribed by . . .

    A   Statements of Standard Accounting Practice (SSAPs).

    B   The UK Companies Acts.

    C   Financial Reporting Standards (FRSs).

    D   The Companies Registration Office.

41.39 Shareholders must be provided with the financial statements of any company in which they own shares because . . .

    A   of the provisions of the Companies Acts.

    B   of regulations issued by the Stock Exchange.

    C   of regulations issued by the Accounting Standards Board (ASB).

    D   None of the above.

Section 42

Purchase of Existing Partnership and Sole Traders' Businesses

If you have difficulty with any of the questions in this section, you should refer to Chapter 42 of **Frank Wood's Business Accounting 1** *(Seventh edition)*

42.1 In relation to the purchase of a business, when the purchase price exceeds the values ascribed to the assets taken over, the difference is known as . . .

    A   goodwill.

    B   a capital reserve.

    C   an error.

    D   None of the above.

42.2 In relation to the purchase of a business, when the purchase price is less than the values ascribed to the assets taken over, the difference is known as . . .

    A   goodwill.

    B   a capital reserve.

    C   an error.

    D   None of the above.

Section 43

Cash Flow Statements: An Introduction

If you have difficulty with any of the questions in this section, you should refer to Chapter 43 of **Frank Wood's Business Accounting 1** *(Seventh edition)*

43.1 An increase in a company's bank overdraft over the course of an accounting period could be explained by . . .

    A   an increase in the company's fixed assets.

    B   an increase in a long-term bank loan.

    C   a decrease in the company's debtors.

    D   an increase in the company's creditors.

43.2 The primary purpose of preparing a cash flow statement for an entity is to provide information about . . .

    A   the profitability or otherwise of its business operations for a period of time.

    B   its financial position at the end of an accounting period.

    C   its cash receipts and cash payments during an accounting period.

    D   None of the above.

43.3 Cash flow statements are required by . . .

    A   the Companies Acts.

    B   Financial Reporting Standard No. 1 (FRS1).

    C   the Stock Exchange.

    D   None of the above.

43.4 Cash flow statements are required for . . .

    A   private companies only.

    B   all entities whose financial statements are intended to give a true and fair view of their profit or loss and financial position, except the published financial statements of 'small' and 'medium-sized' private companies.

    C   public limited companies only.

    D   companies whose shares are traded on a recognised stock exchange only.

43.5 In a firm's cash flow statement, which of the following would appear as a cash inflow ?

    A   The repayment of a bank loan.

    B   The depreciation charge for the current year.

    C   Money received as a result of selling fixed assets.

    D   The difference between the old and new valuations in the case of the revaluation of fixed assets.

43.6 In a cash flow statement, which of the following would appear as a cash outflow ?

    A   The payment for shares in a company whose shares are traded on a Stock Exchange.

    B   A decrease in trade debtors over the course of an accounting period.

    C   Money received as a result of issuing new shares.

    D   None of the above.

43.7 A firm may earn profit during an accounting period but have less money in the bank at the end of the period than it had at the beginning. Which of the following, on its own, could explain this ?

    A   Not paying invoices received from creditors.

    B   The sale of fixed assets during the period.

    C   An increase in trade debtors over the course of the period.

    D   An increase in the depreciation charge relative to the previous accounting period.

43.8 A firm may incur a loss during an accounting period but have more money in its bank account at the end of the period than it had at the beginning. Which of the following, on its own, could explain this apparent contradiction ?

    A   Raising a new long-term loan.

    B   An increase in trade debtors over the course of the period.

    C   An increase in the value of stocks over the course of the period.

    D   Paying trade creditors more quickly this period than in previous accounting periods.

43.9 When preparing a cash flow statement, which of the following would be classified as an operating activity ?

    A   Dividends paid.

    B   A new long-term loan taken out to finance the purchase of fixed assets.

    C   Interest paid on a long-term bank loan.

    D   None of the above.

43.10 When preparing a cash flow statement which of the following would be classified as an investing activity ?

    A   Dividends paid.

    B   A new long-term loan taken out to finance the purchase of fixed assets.

    C   Interest paid on a long-term bank loan.

    D   The cost of purchasing a patent.

43.11 When preparing a cash flow statement, which of the following should be included under the heading 'financing' ?

    A   Dividends paid.

    B   A new long-term loan taken out to finance the purchase of fixed assets.

    C   Interest paid on a long-term bank loan.

    D   The cost of purchasing a patent.

43.12 On a cash flow statement, the net amount of the sub-totals for each of the five main sections (Operating Activities, Returns on Investments and Servicing of Finance, Taxation, Investing Activities and Financing) is equal to the increase or decrease in . . .

    A   cash.

    B   cash and cash equivalents.

    C   working capital.

    D   short-term investments.

43.13 'Cash equivalents', as defined in FRS1, includes . . .

    A   debtors.

    B   long-term investments.

    C   certain short-term investments.

    D   None of the above.

43.14 In general, in order to determine how net investing activities have been financed, it is best to focus on which of the following sections of the cash flow statement ?

    A   Operating activities and financing activities.

    B   Investing activities and financing activities.

    C   Operating activities.

    D   Financing activities.

43.15 When preparing a cash flow statement, the repayment of a loan during the year should be included under the heading . . .

    A   'Operating Activities'.

    B   'Financing'.

    C   'Investing Activities'.

    D   None of the above

43.16 In a cash flow statement, a bonus (scrip) issue of shares should . . .

    A   be shown as a cash inflow arising from investing activities.

    B   be shown as a cash inflow arising from financing.

    C   be shown as a cash outflow.

    D   not be shown at all.

43.17 When preparing a cash flow statement for an accounting period, any change in working capital, excluding balances of cash and cash equivalents, over the course of that accounting period . . .

    A   should be shown under the heading 'financing'.

    B   should be shown as part of the reconciliation of the operating profit or loss to the net cash flow from operating activities.

    C   should not be shown at all.

    D   None of the above.

43.18 In a cash flow statement, money received as a result of a rights issue of ordinary shares should . . .

    A   be shown as a cash inflow.

    B   not be shown at all.

    C   be shown as part of the reconciliation of the operating profit or loss to the net cash flow from operating activities.

    D   None of the above.

43.19 Which of the following should be included in the reconciliation of operating profit or loss to the net cash flow from operating activities ?

    A   A loss incurred on the sale of long-term investments.

    B   A provision for doubtful debts.

    C   An increase in the valuation of fixed assets arising from a revaluation.

    D   An adjustment made to write-down the valuation of stocks to net realisable value.

43.20 When preparing a cash flow statement, which of the following should *not* be included as a cash inflow ?

    A   An increase in the share premium account.

    B   Proceeds arising from the issue of debentures.

    C   An increase in authorised share capital.

    D   Proceeds arising from the issue of new preference shares.

Section 44

An Introduction to the Analysis and Interpretation of Accounting Statements

If you have difficulty with any of the questions in this section, you should refer to Chapter 44 of **Frank Wood's Business Accounting 1** *(Seventh edition)*

44.1 The current ratio is primarily an indication of an entity's . . .

    A   current and future level of profitability.

    B   current level of efficiency.

    C   short-term liquidity.

    D   growth potential.

44.2 The acid-test ratio is calculated as:

A	Current assets	:	Current liabilities
B	Debtors	:	Creditors
C	Current assets less debtors	:	Current liabilities
D	Current assets less stock	:	Current liabilities

44.3 Which of the following should be included in the calculation of the acid-test ratio at a particular date ?

    A   Stock at that date.

    B   Debentures at that date.

    C   Trade creditors at that date.

    D   None of the above.

44.4 The following data was extracted from the accounting records of a business at 31 December.

Total current assets	£ 60,000
Stock	10,000
Debtors	20,000
Total current liabilities	20,000
Creditors	8,000

The acid-test ratio for the business at that date is:

    A   2.5 : 1

    B   3.0 : 1

    C   5.0 : 1

    D   6.0 : 1

44.5 In the case of a sole trader, Return on Capital Employed (ROCE) for an accounting period should be computed as . . .

    A   net profit for the period, less any drawings during that time, as a percentage of the average capital during the period (average capital being calculated as the capital at the beginning of the period plus the capital at the end of the period, divided by two).

    B   gross profit for the period as a percentage of the average capital during the period (average capital being calculated as in answer A above).

    C   net profit for the period as a percentage of the average capital during the period (average capital being calculated as in answers A and B above).

    D   gross profit for the period, less any drawings during that time, as a percentage of the average capital during the period (average capital being calculated as in answers A, B and C above).

44.6 The average number of days which an entity takes to pay its creditors during an accounting period is calculated as . . .

    A   the average of its creditors during that period divided by the total of its credit purchases for that period x 365.

    B   (the average of its creditors during that period divided by the total of its credit purchases for that period) x 365.

    C   the total of its credit purchases for that period divided by the average of its creditors during that period x 365.

    D   (the total of its credit purchases for that period divided by the average of its creditors during that period) x 365.

where, in all cases, average creditors equals the sum of creditors at the beginning of the accounting period and creditors at the end of the accounting period, divided by two.

44.7 During 1996, 78% of a company's sales, which are of a seasonal nature, were made on credit. Given this, the average debtors' collection period (in days) for the company should be calculated as . . .

    A   (the average of its debtors during the year divided by the total of its credit sales for the year) x 365.

    B   (the average of its debtors during the year x 365) divided by the total of its sales for the year.

    C   (the total of its debtors at the end of the year x 365) divided by the total of its sales for the year.

    D   (the total of its credit sales for the year x 365) divided by the average of its debtors during the year.

where, in all cases, average debtors equals the sum of debtors at the beginning of the accounting period and debtors at the end of the accounting period, divided by two.

44.8 The following information relates to a business' most recent accounting period.

Sales for the period	£ 250,000
Purchases during the period	200,000
Stock at the beginning of the period	25,000
Stock at the end of the period	35,000

The business' rate of stock turnover for the period was:

- A 5.43 times
- B 6.33 times
- C 6.67 times
- D 8.33 times

44.9 If a company's gearing ratio is 3 : 5, then its loan capital, as a percentage of its total capital, is:

- A 37.5%
- B 40.0%
- C 60.0%
- D 62.5%

44.10 The abbreviation 'EPS' means . . .

- A Earning Profit Slowly.
- B Exceptionally Profitable Sales.
- C Earnings Per Share.
- D None of the above.

44.11 A company's earnings per share for an accounting period is calculated as . . .

- A the amount of its profit for that period which is available to its ordinary shareholders, divided by the number of ordinary shares it has issued.
- B the total amount of its retained profits, divided by the number of shares it has issued.
- C the amount of its profit for that period, after interest, divided by the number of shares it has issued.
- D None of the above.

44.12 During an accounting period, a company earned a profit, after tax, of £480,000. Its capital was as follows.

Ordinary share capital (£1 shares)	£ 200,000
12% preference share capital (£1 shares)	40,000
10% debentures	60,000

The company's earnings per share for the period was:

  A   £2.00

  B   £2.376

  C   £2.40

  D   None of the above.

44.13 The following data relates to a firm's first year of trading, ended on 31 December.

Current assets at 31 December:	
Stock	£ 10,000
Debtors	5,000
Other current assets	35,000
	50,000
Current liabilities at 31 December	£25,000
Rate of stock turnover during the year	7 times
Average value of stock on hand during the year	£10,000
Sales for the year (all on credit)	£84,000

The firm's acid-test ratio, at 31 December, is:

  A   1.4 : 1

  B   1.6 : 1

  C   1.8 : 1

  D   2.0 : 1

44.14 The following data relates to a firm's first year of trading, ended on 31 December.

Value of stock on hand at 31 December	£10,000
Rate of stock turnover during the year	7 times
Average value of stock on hand during the year	£10,000

The total of the firm's purchases during the year amounted to:

- A £60,000
- B £70,000
- C £80,000
- D £87,000

44.15 The following data relates to a firm's first year of trading, ended on 31 December.

Current assets at 31 December:		
Stock		£ 20,000
Debtors		5,000
Other current assets		25,000
		50,000
Current liabilities at 31 December		35,000
Average stock during the year		12,000
Sales for the year (all on credit)		84,000

The average period of credit given to customers during the year, to the nearest day, was:

- A 12 days
- B 17 days
- C 22 days
- D None of the above.

44.16 The following information has been extracted from the accounts of a wholesaler whose accounting year-end is 31 December.

	1996	1995
Sales	£ 1,000,000	£ 700,000
Gross Profit	300,000	200,000
Stock at 31 December	210,000	190,000

The firm's average rate of stock turnover during 1996 was:

- A 2.98 times
- B 3.06 times
- C 3.33 times
- D 3.50 times

44.17 The following information has been extracted from the accounts of a firm.

	1996	1995
Sales	£ 1,000,000	£ 800,000
Trade debtors	218,500	172,500
Trade creditors	254,000	188,000

85% of the firm's sales, and all of the firm's purchases, are made on credit. The figures given for trade debtors and trade creditors are inclusive of VAT at the rate of 15%.

The average collection period for the firm during 1996 (to the nearest day) was:

- A 73 days
- B 74 days
- C 84 days
- D 94 days

44.18 The following information has been extracted from the accounts of a firm whose accounting year-end is 31 December.

	1996	1995
Sales	£ 900,000	£ 800,000
Gross Profit	200,000	180,000
Trade debtors at 31 December	237,500	218,000
Stock at 31 December	185,000	165,000
Trade creditors at 31 December	230,000	184,000

All of the firm's sales and purchases are made on credit. The figures given for trade debtors and trade creditors are inclusive of VAT at the rate of 15%.

The firm's average creditors payment period during 1996 (to the nearest day) was:

- A 91 days
- B 102 days
- C 105 days
- D 108 days

44.19 The current market value of a company's ordinary shares is £4.00 per share. The company's EPS for the most recent accounting period is 32p and its dividend cover is 2. The dividend yield to the company's ordinary shareholders is:

- A 2%
- B 4%
- C 8%
- D 10%

44.20 A firm's interest cover for an accounting period is calculated as . . .

    A (its net profit for the period less its interest expense for the period) divided by its interest expense for the period.

    B (its net profit for the period plus its interest expense for the period) divided by its interest expense for the period.

    C (its net profit for the period, before tax, plus its interest expense for the period) divided by its interest expense for the period.

    D its net profit for the period divided by its interest expense for the period.

44.21 Which of the following is most useful when attempting to establish whether a business' level of profitability and its financial position have improved or deteriorated relative to competitors in the same industry ?

    A Rule-of-thumb measures.

    B Measures of the past performance of the business.

    C Measures of both the past and current performances of the business.

    D Industry average measures.

44.22 The accuracy of the profit figure shown in the profit and loss account of a business may be affected by . . .

    A the countries in which the business operates.

    B the accounting methods which the business uses.

    C the industry in which the business operates.

    D None of the above.

44.23 An increase in a company's working capital over the course of an accounting period could be explained by . . .

    A the purchase of fixed assets on credit during the period.

    B the purchase of fixed assets by cheque during the period.

    C the expansion of operations during the period.

    D None of the above.

44.24 If the total of a firm's current liabilities exceeds that of its current assets (including a bank balance of £3,000) a payment of £1,000 to a creditor, by cheque will cause the firm's current ratio to . . .

    A increase.

    B decrease.

    C remain the same.

    D It is not possible to tell, as the information given is insufficient.

44.25 After proposing a final dividend of £50,000, a company which has a £60,000 positive bank balance had a current ratio of 1.5 : 1. If the company uses its bank balance to pay the dividend, its current ratio will . . .

   A   increase.

   B   decrease.

   C   remain the same.

   D   It is not possible to tell, as the information given is insufficient.

44.26 After proposing a final dividend of £50,000, a company which has a £60,000 bank balance had a current ratio of 1.5 : 1 and an acid-test ratio of 0.7 : 1. If the company uses its bank balance to pay the dividend, its acid-test ratio will . . .

   A   decrease.

   B   increase.

   C   remain the same.

   D   It is not possible to tell, as the information given is insufficient.

44.27 A business which had £10,000 in its bank current account purchased and paid for stock costing £2,000. As a result of this transaction, the business' current ratio . . .

   A   remains the same.

   B   improves.

   C   disimproves.

   D   It is not possible to tell from the information given.

44.28 A business purchased stock for £2,000 and paid for it by cheque on the same day. If, prior to buying the stock, the business had £4,000 in its bank account, the effect of this transaction on its acid-test ratio is:

   A   The acid-test ratio disimproves.

   B   The acid-test ratio improves.

   C   The acid-test ratio remains the same.

   D   It is not possible to tell from the information given.

44.29 When a business purchases stock on credit its acid-test ratio . . .

   A   increases.

   B   remains the same.

   C   decreases.

   D   It is not possible to tell from the information given.

44.30 When a business purchases stock on credit its current ratio . . .

    A   increases.

    B   does not change.

    C   decreases.

    D   It is not possible to tell from the information given as the current ratio may increase, decrease or remain unchanged depending on the size of the purchase.

Section 45

Accounting Theory

If you have difficulty with any of the questions in this section, you should refer to Chapter 45 of **Frank Wood's Business Accounting 1** *(Seventh edition)*

45.1 The 'inductive' approach to accounting theory . . .

    A   seeks to improve accounting practice rather than base a set of rules on what is currently being done.

    B   involves observing and analysing the practices of accountants to see if any consistent behaviour can be detected and converted into rules.

    C   looking at what is done in other countries and selecting what are considered to be the best practices there.

    D   None of the above.

45.2 The 'normative' approach to accounting theory . . .

    A   involves observing and analysing the practices of accountants to see if any consistent behaviour can be detected and converted into rules.

    B   seeks to improve accounting practice rather than base a set of rules on what is currently being done.

    C   looking at what is done in other countries and selecting what are considered to be the best practices there.

    D   None of the above.

45.3 The historical cost of an item is . . .

    A   the same as its net book value.

    B   the amount which it originally cost.

    C   the amount it would now cost to replace it.

    D   None of the above.

Answers & Explanations

The answer to each question is given immediately after the question number. This is then followed by an explanation of the answer including, in many cases, an explanation of why the other answers presented are not correct.

The Accounting Equation and the Balance Sheet

1.1	A	Machinery is an asset because it is a resource, from which benefits can be derived (through use).
	B	Money owed by a firm to one of its suppliers is a liability (obligation) whether owed in respect of goods purchased on credit or owed for any other reason.
	C	An overdrawn balance on a firm's bank account is a liability, as it represents an obligation on the part of the business to repay that money to a bank.
	D	The capital of a firm is not an asset as it represents money owed by the business to the proprietor of the business.
1.2	D	Liabilities are obligations to pay amounts of money.
	A	A building owned by the firm is an asset (resource).
	B	Cash in the firm's safe is an asset (resource).
	C	Money owed to the firm by its debtors is an asset (resource).
1.3	D	As per the Accounting Equation.
1.4	A	As per the Accounting Equation, Capital = Assets - Liabilities. The figures given in answers B, C and D will not satisfy this equation.

1.5 B According to the Accounting Equation, Capital = Assets - Liabilities.

Assets
Premises owned by the firm		£ 20,000
Stock owned by the firm		8,500
Cash in the firm's safe		100
		28,600

Liabilities
Money owed by the firm to its creditors	£ 3,000	
Loan received by the firm from a bank	4,000	- 7,000
Capital (= Assets - Liabilities)		21,600

1.6 A The firm has less money in its bank account than it previously had because it has just paid some of the money it had there to one of its creditors. It also owes less because the money it has just paid out of its bank account has been used to settle a debt which it previously owed.

   B This double entry is not the correct way to record any transaction. This is because a firm's bank balance will be increased as a result of it lodging money and its creditors will be increased as a result of it purchasing something on credit. As no single transaction gives rise to both of these effects, no single transaction should be recorded in this way.

   C This double entry is not the correct way to record any transaction. This is because a firm's bank balance will be reduced as a result of it withdrawing money or issuing a cheque and its creditors will be increased as a result of it purchasing something on credit. As no single transaction gives rise to both of these effects, no single transaction should be recorded in this way. Furthermore, recording any transaction correctly will result in one asset (or liability) being increased and another reduced or an asset (liability) being increased (decreased) and a liability (asset) also being increased (decreased). In this case, an asset is being decreased and a liability is being increased - this cannot be correct.

1.7	B	As a result of a firm lodging money received from one of its debtors the firm has more money than it previously had and is owed less than it previously was.
		A This is the correct double-entry to record a cheque paid to a creditor.
		C This double entry is not the correct way to record any transaction. This is because a firm's cash balance will be increased as a result of it receiving cash and its loan balance will be decreased as a result of it paying off some of that loan, either in cash or by cheque. As no single transaction gives rise to both of these effects, no single transaction should be recorded in this way. Furthermore, recording any transaction correctly will result in one asset (or liability) being increased and another reduced or an asset (liability) being increased (decreased) and a liability (asset) also being increased (decreased). In this case, an asset is being increased and a liability is being decreased - this cannot be correct.
		D This double entry is not the correct way to record any transaction. This is because a firm's stock will be increased as a result of it buying stock, either for cash or on credit and its capital will be decreased as a result of the proprietor taking money, or other assets, out of the firm or by the firm incurring a loss. As no single transaction gives rise to both of these effects, no single transaction should be recorded in this way. Furthermore, recording any transaction correctly will result in one asset (or liability) being increased and another reduced or an asset (liability) being increased (decreased) and a liability (asset) also being increased (decreased). In this case, an asset is being increased and a liability (Capital is a special kind of liability) is being decreased - this cannot be correct.
1.8	C	The effect of a firm being granted a bank loan and the amount of the loan being transferred into its bank current account is that it now has more money in its bank current account than it previously had and it owes more money than it previously did.
		A This is the correct double-entry to record the firm paying off some, or all, of its loan.
		B This double entry is not the correct way to record any transaction. This is because a firm's bank balance will be decreased as a result of it making a payment and its loan balance will be increased as a result of it borrowing more, thereby increasing its bank balance. As no single transaction gives rise to both of these effects, no single transaction should be recorded in this way. Furthermore, recording any transaction correctly will result in one asset (or liability) being increased and another reduced or an asset (liability) being increased (decreased) and a liability (asset) also being increased (decreased). In this case, an asset is being decreased and a liability is being increased - this cannot be correct.
1.9	D	A This is the correct double entry to record a cheque paid to a creditor.
		B This is not the correct way to record any transaction because it is contrary to the double entry rule. Recording any transaction correctly will result in one asset (or liability) being increased and another reduced or an asset (liability) being increased (decreased) and a liability (asset) also being increased (decreased). In this case, an asset is being increased and no other asset is being reduced nor is a liability being increased.
		C This double entry is not the correct way to record any transaction. This is because a firm's cash balance will be increased as a result of it receiving cash whereas its loan balance will be decreased as a result of it paying money. As no single transaction gives rise to both of these effects (money coming in and money going out are two separate transactions), no single transaction should be recorded in this way. Furthermore, recording any transaction correctly will result in one asset (or liability) being increased and another reduced or an asset (liability) being increased (decreased) and a liability (asset) also being increased (decreased). In this case, an asset is being increased and a liability is being decreased - this cannot be correct.

The Double-Entry System for Assets, Liabilities and Capital

2.1	A	B	To record a decrease in capital the capital account must be debited.
		C	To record an increase in any given liability account that account must be credited.
		D	To record a decrease in any given liability account that account must be debited.
2.2	B		This is the double entry record required when a firm buys a vehicle and pays for it by cheque.
		A	The recording of a transaction in the double-entry accounting records involves debiting one ledger account and crediting another, not debiting and crediting the same account. If the business in question has two separate accounts in a bank, for example, a deposit account and a current account, it should have a separate 'T' account in its ledger for each. Therefore, even a transfer of money from one bank account to the other would necessitate debiting and crediting two different ledger accounts.
2.3	A	B	This is the correct way for a school to record the sale of a computer and lodgement of the proceeds.
		C	This is the correct way for a school to record the sale of a computer for cash.
		D	This is the correct way for a school to record the purchase of a computer for cash.
2.4	B	A	When money is lodged, the bank account should be debited, not credited. Also, a debit entry in a debtor's account increases the balance on that account. As this balance should be reduced when money is received from a debtor, this account should be credited.
		C	This is the correct double-entry to record the lodgement of cash on hand.
		D	This is the correct double-entry to record the receipt of money from P. Doyle, a debtor, which is not lodged.
2.5	C	A	Lodging money into a bank account will increase the balance on that account. Recording such an increase in an asset account requires a debit entry in that account. Also, the capital account (being a type of liability) always has a credit balance. Therefore, to record an increase in that account, the account must be credited.
		B	This is the correct double-entry to record the introduction of new capital in the form of cash, where that cash has not yet been lodged.
		D	Lodging money into the bank account will increase the balance on that account but will not affect the cash account. Introducing capital in the form of cash, and not lodging it, would increase the cash account - which would require a debit entry in that account. Also, the capital account (being a type of liability) always has a credit balance. Therefore, to record an increase in that account, the account must be credited.
2.6	D	A	This is the correct double-entry to record cash paid to B. Lee, a creditor.
		B	Making a payment by cheque will reduce the amount of money in the bank account. Therefore, the bank account, being an asset, must be credited.
		C	All payments by cheque should be recorded in the bank account, not the cash account.

The Asset of Stock

3.1   C   In accounting, the meaning of the term 'purchases' is limited to the purchase of goods which are intended to be resold in the normal course of business, hopefully at a profit. It does not matter whether the goods are paid for or not. Certain items bought (for example, a car bought by an accountancy firm) are not 'purchases', as they are not intended to be resold in the normal course of business. However, cars bought by a garage would normally be included in 'purchases' as the garage would have bought them with the intention of re-selling them.

         A   This is incorrect as 'all items bought' could include items not intended to be for resale

         B   This answer is incorrect because the term 'purchases' means goods bought with the intention of being re-sold, whether bought for cash or on credit.

         D   This answer is incorrect because the term 'purchases' means goods bought with the intention of being re-sold, whether paid for (cash purchase) or not (credit purchase).

3.2   D   In accounting, the term 'sales' means the sale of goods originally acquired for the purpose of being resold, whether sold for cash or on credit. In the case of a newsagent, office furniture would not have been acquired for this purpose.

         A   In the case of a newsagent, the sale of office furniture, whether sold for cash or on credit, should not be included in the sales figure as the furniture would not have been acquired with the intention of being re-sold.

         B   As for answer A above.

         C   As for answer A above.

3.3   A   The account for R. Webb, being a debtor's account, is an asset account. As a result of selling goods on credit to R. Webb, he now owes more than he previously did. To increase the amount in the asset account, that account must be debited.

         The sale of goods is always recorded in the sales account - and always as a credit entry.

         B   This answer (Debit the returns inwards account and credit R. Webb's account) is the correct double-entry to record the return of goods by R. Webb.

         C   This answer (Debit the cash account and credit the purchases account) is not the correct double-entry to record any transaction because the purchases account is always debited. The opposite entry, debit the purchases account and credit the cash account, is the correct way to record the purchase of goods for cash.

         D   Debit R. Webb's account and credit the returns inwards account, being the opposite of answer B, is not the correct double-entry to record any transaction.

3.4   B   Having returned some goods, S. James, a credit customer (the same as a debtor) now owes less than he previously did. As the amount owed by a debtor is an asset and an asset account has to be credited to reduce it, S. James' account has to be credited. Returns inwards, being the opposite of sales (which is always credited), has to be debited.

         A   Debit the sales account and credit K. Bryan's account is not the correct double-entry to record any transaction. This is because all entries in the sales account should be on the credit side and the account containing the investment by the owner (proprietor), K. Bryan, is called the capital account.

         C   Debit the sales account and credit S. James' account is not the correct double-entry to record any transaction. This is because all entries in the sales account should be on the credit side. This entry is the opposite to that required to record a credit sale to S. James.

         D   Debit S. James' account and credit the returns inwards account is not the correct double-entry to record any transaction. This is because all entries in the returns inwards account should be on the debit side.

3.5 B Having returned some goods, K. Bryan, a credit customer (the same as a debtor) now owes less than he previously did. As the amount owed by a debtor is an asset and an asset account has to be credited to reduce it, K. Bryan's account has to be credited. Returns inwards, being the opposite of sales (which is always credited), has to be debited.

   A Debit the sales account and credit K. Bryan's account is not the correct double-entry to record any transaction. This is because all entries in the sales account should be on the credit side. This entry is the opposite to that required to record a credit sale to K. Bryan.

   C Debit the sales account and credit S. James' account is not the correct double-entry to record any transaction. This is because all entries in the sales account should be on the credit side and the account for the investment by the owner (proprietor), S. James, is called the capital account.

   D Debit S. James' account and credit the returns inwards account is not the correct double-entry to record any transaction. This is because all entries in the returns inwards account should be on the debit side and the account for the investment by the owner (proprietor), S. James, is called the capital account.

3.6 C Entries in the purchases account are always on the debit side. Having paid cash to D. Connolly, W. Balfe now has less cash. This reduction in this asset has to be recorded as a credit entry in the cash account.

   A Debit the sales account and credit W. Balfe's account is not the correct double-entry to record any transaction. This is because all entries in the sales account should be on the credit side and the account for the owner (proprietor), W. Balfe, is called the capital account.

   B Neither of the accounts 'A. O'Dea' or 'returns inwards' are relevant to this transaction as the transaction is a purchase, not a return, and the only people involved are W. Balfe and D. Connolly. Debit the returns inwards account and credit A. O'Dea's account is the correct double-entry to record goods returned by A. O'Dea.

   D Debit D. Connolly's account and credit the returns inwards account is not the correct double-entry to record any transaction. This is because all entries in the returns inwards account should be on the debit side.

3.7 D As A. Miller is a creditor, A. Miller's account is a liability. As a result of returning goods to him, he is now owed less. This reduction in a liability has to be recorded by a debit entry. Entries in the returns outwards account are always on the credit side.

   A Debit the sales account and credit A. Miller's account is not the correct double-entry to record any transaction. This is because all entries in the sales account should be on the credit side.

   B Debit the returns inwards account and credit A. Miller's account is the correct double-entry to record goods returned *by* A. Miller.

   C Debit the cash account and credit the purchases account is not the correct double-entry to record any transaction. This is because all entries in the purchases account should be on the debit side.

The Effect of Profit or Loss on Capital and the Double-Entry System for Expenses and Revenues

4.1 D A Earning profit increases capital.

   B Earning profit increases capital. Incurring losses would reduce capital.

   C In addition to arising from profit being earned, the capital of a firm can arise, or be increased, by the proprietor introducing value into the business - in the form of money or other assets. Capital will be reduced by the proprietor taking such value out of the business.

4.2	C	A	Only the sale of 'goods' should be recorded in the sales account (as a credit). There should be a separate account for hire purchase commission.
		B	Debit the sales account and credit the bank account is not the correct double-entry to record any transaction. This is because all entries in the sales account should be on the credit side. Furthermore, lodgements should be recorded on the debit side of the bank account.
4.3	B		All expenses are recorded as debit entries in the relevant expense account. The bank balance is being reduced and, as the bank balance is an asset and reductions in assets are recorded by a credit entry, the entry in the bank account has to be a credit.
		A	A debit entry in the bank account means that money has been lodged. In this transaction money is being paid by cheque.
		C	The cost of rates should be recorded in the rates account and the cost of each other expense item should be recorded in an account specifically for that expense item. In this way, the ledger provides detailed information on how much each expense has cost. If all expenses were recorded in a single 'expenses' account, the ledger would only show how much expenses in total cost and not how much each individual type of expense cost.
4.4	C		All expenses are recorded as a debit entry in the relevant expense account. The bank balance is being reduced by paying a cheque and, as the bank balance is an asset and reductions in assets are recorded by a credit entry, the entry in the bank account has to be a credit.
		A	A debit entry in the bank account means that money has been lodged. In this transaction money is being paid by cheque.
		B	Payments by cheque, as opposed to cash, should be credited in the bank account, not the cash account.

Balancing Off Accounts

5.1 B

P. Kelly

May 01	Sales	205	May 17	Bank	300
May 14	Sales	360	May 28	Returns In	50
May 31	Sales	180	*May 31*	*Balance c/d*	395
		745			745

5.2 A

J. Barker

June 02	Sales	200	June 15	Bank	330
June 12	Sales	650	June 19	Balance c/d	520
		850			850
June 20	*Balance b/d*	*520*	June 25	Returns Inwards	75
June 30	Sales	800			

5.3	C	There must be at least one debit entry and at least one credit entry for every transaction and for each transaction the total of the debit entries must equal that of the credit entries. A debit entry is required in order to decrease the balance on a liability account and a credit entry is required in order to decrease the balance on an asset account. As the two decreases are the same amount, the total of the debit entries will equal that of the credit entries.
		A A debit entry is required in order to increase the balance on an asset account. A debit entry is also required in order to decrease the balance on a liability account. As recording any transaction requires at least one debit entry and at least one credit entry and given that the total of the debit entries for a particular transaction must equal that of the credit entries for the same transaction, this answer (two debit entries) cannot be the record of any single transaction.

	B	Two debit entries are required in order to increase the balance on the two asset accounts (one for each account). As recording any transaction requires at least one debit entry and at least one credit entry and given that the total of the debit entries for a particular transaction must equal that of the credit entries for the same transaction, this answer (two debit entries) cannot be the record of any single transaction.
	D	Two credit entries are required in order to decrease the balance on an asset and increase the balance on a liability account. As recording any transaction requires at least one debit entry and at least one credit entry and given that the total of the debit entries for a particular transaction must equal that of the credit entries for the same transaction, this answer (two credit entries) cannot be the record of any single transaction.
5.4 A		This transaction will be recorded by debiting the bank account (thereby increasing the debit balance brought down on it) and crediting N. Taylor's account.
	B	The purchase of stock either for cash or on credit will not affect the bank account in the firm's ledger and the purchase of stock by cheque will *decrease* the debit balance brought down on that account.
	C	The repayment of a loan in cash will not affect the bank account in the firm's ledger and the repayment of a loan by cheque will *decrease* the debit balance brought down on that account.
	D	The payment of cash to one of the firm's creditors will not affect the bank account in the firm's ledger whereas payment by cheque will *decrease* the debit balance brought down on that account.

The Trial Balance

6.1	D	A	The financial position of a firm is shown by its balance sheet.
		B	Although a trial balance which does not balance means that something is wrong, the error may be in the underlying accounting records or in the addition of the figures in the trial balance itself. Even if the trial balance balances, this is not conclusive evidence that everything in the accounting records is correct. There may still be some errors in the double-entry records, for example, errors of omission, compensating errors etc.
		C	The individual entries in the double-entry accounting records are shown in the ledger accounts whereas the balances on these accounts (the net of all of the entries in the individual accounts) are shown in the trial balance.
6.2	A	B	A balanced trial balance does not prove that the double-entry record for all transactions is correct. Even if the trial balance balances, there may be errors in the accounting records, for example, errors of omission, compensating errors etc.
		C	The trial balance does not prove that the balance on *any* individual ledger account is correct.
		D	In order to determine whether an entity has earned a profit or incurred a loss, a profit and loss account, not a trial balance, should be prepared.
6.3	C		The purpose of preparing a trial balance is to establish whether the total of the debit balances brought down in the related nominal (general) ledger equals that of the credit balances brought down. If the trial balance totals do not agree, the underlying accounting records are not correct. Even if they do agree, there may still be some errors in the ledger, for example, errors of omission, compensating errors etc.
6.4	B	A	Entering either the debit entry or the credit entry for a particular transaction in the wrong class of ledger account is an *error of principle*.
		C	Entering a correct figure in the wrong person's account is an *error of commission*.
		D	Two errors, one of which cancels out the other, are known as *a compensating error*.

6.5	C	A Entering either the debit entry or the credit entry for a particular transaction in the wrong class of ledger account is an *error of principle*.
		B Omitting to record a transaction in the double-entry accounting records is an *error of omission*.
6.6	A	An error of principle arises when either the debit entry or the credit entry for a particular transaction is entered in the wrong class of ledger account.
		B Omitting to record a sale (or any other transaction) in the double-entry accounting records is an *error of omission*.
		C Entering a correct figure in the wrong person's account is an *error of commission*.
6.7	C	A Entering either the debit entry or the credit entry for a particular transaction in the wrong class of ledger account is an *error of principle*.
		B Entering a correct figure in the wrong person's account is an *error of commission*.

Trading and Profit and Loss Accounts: An Introduction

7.1	B	A *Gross* profit is determined by preparing a trading account but *net* profit or loss is not.
		C A trial balance is prepared in order to determine whether the total of the debit balances brought down in the related nominal (general) ledger equals that of the credit balances brought down - it is not prepared in order to determine any profit figure.
		D A balance sheet is prepared in order to show the financial position of an entity at a particular point in time, not to determine the profit earned or loss incurred by it over a period of time.
7.2	D	Sales - Cost of Sales = Gross Profit Sales - Cost of Sales = 25% of the Cost of Sales £300,000 - Cost of Sales = 25% of the Cost of Sales £300,000 = Cost of Sales + 25% of the Cost of Sales £300,000 = 125% of the Cost of Sales = Cost of Sales * 1.25 Cost of Sales = £300,000 / 1.25 = £240,000
7.3	C	Net Profit = Gross Profit - Expenses = £35,000 - £18,000 = £17,000 £17,000 = 17% of sales Therefore, Sales = £17,000 / 17 * 100 = £100,000 Cost of Sales = Sales - Gross Profit = £100,000 - £35,000 = £65,000
7.4	A	Capital at the end of a year = capital at the start of the year + net profit for the year + capital introduced during the year - drawings taken during the year. As no information is given regarding capital introduced or drawings, the sole trader's capital at the end of the year cannot be determined. If no capital was introduced and there were no drawings, then the trader's capital at the end of the year would have been £120,000.

Balance Sheets

8.1 C
- A A balance sheet is not a ledger account. The balance brought down on each ledger account is listed in the form of a trial balance, from which a balance sheet may be prepared. The balance brought down on *all* of the ledger accounts should be listed in this way; there is no other ledger account which proves that the accounting records balance.
- B A balance sheet does not show the market value of a firm - it is simply a list, in a particular format, of the balances brought down in a number of the ledger accounts. The market value of a firm is whatever amount it can be sold for. This cannot be shown in the accounting records because it changes all the time.
- D A balance sheet does not show the market value of individual assets or liabilities - it is simply a list, in a particular format, of the balances brought down in a number of the ledger accounts. The market value of a firm's assets and liabilities is whatever amount they can be sold for or whatever amount it would cost the firm to pay them off. These amounts cannot be shown in the accounting records because they change all the time.

8.2 C
- A As a balance sheet shows the financial position of an entity at a particular point in time, rather than covering a period of time, the heading on it has to include the date in question.
- B As for answer A above.
- D The financial position must be shown as at a specific point in time - 'December' is not a specific moment in time, whereas the close of business on 31 December is.

8.3 C
- A A balance sheet of a firm does not show the nature of that firm's business.
- B A balance sheet of a firm does not provide any information concerning who the owners of the firm are.
- D The extent to which a balance sheet shows the physical size of a firm is limited to the figures given in it for individual assets and liabilities. These figures alone are not sufficient to determine the physical size of a firm. No information is given regarding, for example, the size of manufacturing facilities, the number of retail outlets etc.

8.4 B
- A A firm's fixed assets are those assets which have an expected useful economic life of more than one year and were purchased by it for continuing use in its business, rather than for resale. Fixed assets do not have to be of substantial value.
- C While many fixed assets have a physical substance (known as tangible fixed assets) there are fixed assets which do not, for example, patents and trade marks (known as intangible fixed assets).

8.5 B
- A Money receivable within a year, for example, from debtors, is a current asset. However, there are other types of current assets also, for example, cash already on hand and stock.
- C Current assets can comprise more than just debtors, stock and cash and bank balances.
- D The total of current assets is likely to comprise much more than just debtors, for example, cash, stock and money in the bank.

8.6 C
- A Amounts payable by the firm within six months of the date of the balance sheet date are current liabilities - as current liabilities are amounts payable within one year of the balance sheet date.
- B Amounts payable by the firm within nine months of the date of the balance sheet date are current liabilities - as current liabilities are amounts payable within one year of the balance sheet date.

8.7	B	A	Any amount payable by the firm within one year of its balance sheet date is a current liability. For example, in addition to overdrafts and loans, money owed to creditors in respect of goods purchased on credit is a current liability.
		C	As for answer A above.
		D	Liabilities which were incurred by the firm in the six months prior to the date of the balance sheet could already have been discharged and, if not, could be either current liabilities or long-term liabilities, depending on when they are due to be discharged.
8.8	D	*Item 1*	A bank loan repayable by the firm as a single lump sum on 31 March 1998 is a long-term liability, as 31 March 1998 is more than one year after 31 December 1996.
		Item 2	An electricity bill relating to November and December 1996 but unpaid as at 31 December 1996, is a current liability as the bill is due to be paid within one year of 31 December 1996. (Although this is not stated, it should be apparent that this is necessary in order to maintain a supply of electricity.)
		Item 3	The portion of a five year bank loan due to be paid by the firm in 1997 is a current liability as at 31 December 1996, as money due to be paid in 1997 is clearly payable within one year of 31 December 1996.
8.9	A		Capital = Assets - Liabilities (per the Accounting Equation) Therefore, Capital at 1 June = Total of all assets at 1 June - Total of all liabilities at 1 June. = £2,300 - £2,500 = - £200. Capital at 30 June = Capital at 1 June + Capital introduced during June + Net profit earned during June - Drawings during June = - £200 + £5,000 + £1,000 - £700 = £5,100
8.10	B		According to the accounting equation, Capital = Assets - Liabilities. The balance sheet of Firm 2 is the only one in which the figure given for capital is equal to the difference between the total of the assets and the total of the liabilities.
			This question may also be solved by following the principle that the total of the debit balances in a balance sheet (assets) must equal that of the credit balances in the same balance sheet (liabilities and capital). This is true only in the case of Firm 2.
8.11	D		In accordance with the accounting equation, Capital (at any particular date) = Assets (at that date) - Liabilities (at that date). Given that Assets less Liabilities also equals Net Assets, Capital (Assets - Liabilities) must also equal Net Assets.
		A	The sum of fixed assets plus current assets equals total assets. Liabilities have to be deducted from this to get capital.
		B	Current assets have to be added to the total of fixed assets, and then current liabilities have to be deducted from the resulting total to give net assets (the same as capital).
		C	This is a meaningless total. The total amount of capital he has introduced should not be added to the total of net assets.
8.12	D		If a firm is selling exclusively on credit, its stock will be sold on credit, thus becoming debtors. When money is received from debtors, it will be lodged, thereby increasing the bank balance. Cash, by definition, is the most liquid asset.
8.13	C		As no capital has been introduced during the year, Capital at 31 December = Capital at 1 January + Net profit for the year - Drawings during the year. Therefore, Net profit for the year = Capital at 31 December - Capital at 1 January + Drawings during the year = £31,000 - £25,000 + £23,000 = £29,000

8.14   D   Capital = Assets - Liabilities

        A As there is no change in assets (the increased fixed assets are offset by the decreased current assets) and no change in liabilities, capital will not change.

        B The increase in fixed assets is offset by the decrease in liabilities so there is no change in capital.

        C Assets decrease without a corresponding decrease in liabilities. Therefore, capital will be reduced. This decrease in capital is most likely to be due to the payment of an expense.

Trading and Profit and Loss Accounts and Balance Sheets: Further Considerations

9.1   A

        B Although it is correct that carriage inwards should not be shown in the balance sheet, this is not a reason why it should be included in the cost of sales calculation.

        C Although it is correct to include carriage outwards as an expense in the profit and loss account, this is not a reason why carriage inwards should be included in the cost of sales calculation.

9.2   C

Stock at 1 July	£ 1,300
Purchases during July	6,400
Carriage inwards on July purchases	200
Stock at 31 July	- 900
Cost of sales for July	7,000

9.3   A   The cost of bringing goods to a merchantable condition is a cost of sale, which is matched (offset) against the sales figure in the trading account.

9.4   D   Stock at 1 January 1996 = Stock at 31 December 1995.
1996 Cost of Sales (£500,000) = Stock at 1 January 1996 (£150,000) + Purchases during 1996 (missing figure) - Stock at 31 December 1996 (£200,000). Therefore, purchases during 1996, the figure required to solve the equation = £550,000.

9.5   B

        A Any increase in stock over the course of the period would have to have been paid for either in cash or by cheque or else purchased on credit. In all of these cases the cash balance would either not have changed or would have decreased.

        C Assuming that bills are being paid by the sole trader at the normal rate, customers taking longer to pay their bills will, over time, reduce the cash and / or bank balance(s) as money will be paid out at the normal rate but will be coming in at a slower rate.

        D The purchase of fixed assets would have to have been paid for either in cash or by cheque or else purchased on credit. In all of these cases the cash balance would either not have changed or would have decreased.

9.6   D   The term 'purchases' means the purchase of goods intended for, and available for, resale. Once goods which were purchased are taken by the proprietor, they are no longer available for resale. Therefore, the purchases figure should be reduced (credited) so that the balance remaining in the purchases account is the total of goods purchased which are available for sale (or were available and were subsequently sold).

        A Stock purchased and paid for by the proprietor is a sale whereas stock taken by the proprietor, without him paying for it is drawings. A single amount of stock cannot represent both a sale and drawings.

        B There isn't a ledger account for stock.

        C As for answer A above, except that in this case the possible entries are reversed.

9.7	B	The correct double-entry to record stock withdrawn from a firm by the proprietor, without him paying for it, is to debit the drawings account and credit the purchases account. If these entries are not made, then the figure for drawings in the balance sheet will be understated and the purchases figure in the trading account will be overstated, thus overstating the cost of sales and understating both the gross profit and the net profit. The closing stock figure will not be affected as this figure is arrived at as a result of stocktaking at the balance sheet date.
9.8	C	Purchases would be overstated because there would be a debit entry in the purchases account which shouldn't be there. As the purchases figure is one of the components of the cost of sales figure, the cost of sales figure would also be overstated. Therefore, gross profit and consequently net profit would be understated.
		A Purchases (and therefore cost of sales) would be overstated. Therefore, gross profit would be understated.
		B There would not be any effect on the total of expenses.
		D Closing capital (after deducting drawings) would be overstated, because the amount of drawings deducted would be understated (because a debit entry has been omitted from the drawings account).
9.9	B	Amount of the business bank loan = (£53,000 + £6,600) - £25,000 = £34,600. Capital at 1 January = Assets at 1 January - Liabilities at 1 January = (£53,000 + £6,600) - £34,600 = £25,000. This £25,000 could also be viewed as Tom's personal interest in the business (the loan he got from his brother). Capital at 31 December = Assets at 31 December - Liabilities at 31 December. This is equal to net assets at 31 December = £37,200. But, Capital at 31 December = Capital at 1 January + Net profit for the year - Drawings during the year. Therefore, £37,200 = £25,000 + £21,100 - Drawings during the year. Therefore, drawings during the year = £8,900.
9.10	A	Stocktaking means counting the quantity of each item in stock, valuing each item individually and adding all of the individual values together to get the total value of stock.
		B There isn't a stock account in the nominal (general) ledger.
		C Sales - Purchases is not equal to stock.
		D Sales - Cost of Sales = Gross Profit (not the value of stock).

Accounting Concepts

10.1	C	A The going concern concept is concerned with the existence (survival) of a firm, not its profitability. Obviously a firm will not survive if it repeatedly incurs losses over the long-term. However, many firms incur losses on an occasional basis but remain in business because of the more frequent years in which they earn profits.
		B The going concern concept is concerned with the foreseeable future, not with eternity.
		D A firm which is not expected to be able to continue operating is not a going concern, and therefore, the going concern concept should not be applied in this case.
10.2	C	A is the prudence concept.
		B is the consistency concept.
		D is the accruals concept.
10.3	C	A A sole trader has access to the assets of his business. He can withdraw cash, stock etc. These withdrawals are shown in his accounts as drawings.
		B Although it is true that accounts have to be prepared for every firm - for example, for tax purposes, this is not because of the entity concept.

10.4	C	A	is the consistency concept.
		B	is one aspect of the prudence concept. The other aspect is that losses should be provided for as soon as they are foreseen.
10.5	C	A	It is true that the accruals concept applies to revenues and expenses but not exclusively so - it also applies to assets and liabilities.
		B	It is true that the accruals concept applies to assets and liabilities but not exclusively so - it also applies to revenues and expenses.
		D	The accruals concept is one of the fundamental accounting concepts, that is, those concepts referred to in SSAP 2.
10.6	A	B	An accounting period may be, but does not have to be, a calendar year.
		C	An accounting period can be of any duration. However, for tax purposes, as opposed to accounting purposes, accounts must be prepared for periods not exceeding 12 months.
10.7	B	A	is the accruals concept.
		C	is the consistency concept.
10.8	A	B	The consistency concept requires consistency of treatment over time not across firms.
		C	Firms may change the way in which they prepare their accounts if the new way is more 'correct' than the old.
10.9	C	A	Although the materiality concept is a well-recognised accounting concept, it is not one of the 'fundamental' accounting concepts referred to in SSAP2.
		B	Although the business entity concept is a well-recognised accounting concept, it is not one of the 'fundamental' accounting concepts referred to in SSAP2.
		D	Although the money measurement concept is a well-recognised accounting concept, it is not one of the 'fundamental' accounting concepts referred to in SSAP2.
10.10	C	A	The financial statements of a firm should be prepared on the basis that the firm is a going concern, only when this is considered to be the case. If it is considered that the firm is not a going concern, its accounts should be prepared on that basis. This will mean that assets will be shown at their market value, provision will have to be made for redundancy costs, costs associated with selling assets etc. and all liabilities will be shown as current liabilities (as the firm is unlikely to be in business after more than one year to pay long-term liabilities).
		B	Although the materiality concept is a well-recognised accounting concept, it is not one of the 'fundamental' accounting concepts referred to in SSAP2.
10.11	A		The matching concept is often known as the accruals concept because the accruals concept means that profit is equal to revenues less expenses, that is, expenses are matched (offset) against revenues to give a profit figure.

Books of Original Entry and Ledgers

11.1   B   Books of original entry are so called because they are the first (original) place in which transactions are recorded. They are also known as 'Books of Prime Entry'.

          A   Data is 'posted' to the Sales Ledger from the Sales Journal, the Cash Book and possibly the Journal. Therefore, the Sales Ledger is not the *first* place in which the information in it is recorded.

          C   Data is 'posted' to the general ledger from the Books of Original Entry. Therefore, the General Ledger is not the *first* place in which the information in it is recorded.

          D   Data is 'posted' to the purchases ledger from the Purchases Journal, the Cash Book and possibly the Journal. Therefore, the Purchases Ledger is not the *first* place in which the information in it is recorded.

11.2   C   A   Payments to suppliers are entered in the Cash Book (or Cheque Payments Book).

          B   Invoices are entered in the Purchases Journal (Purchases Daybook) net of trade discount.

          D   Discounts received are entered in the Cash Book (or Cash Receipts Book).

11.3   C   A   Buildings is a real account.

          B   Wages is a nominal account.

11.4   A   B   Postings are made to the nominal (general) ledger from the books of original entry.

          C   Transactions are first recorded in the books of original entry (from which postings are made to the nominal (general) ledger).

11.5   C   A   The first record of a transaction is made in a book of original entry.

          B   'Posting' means transferring data which has already been recorded somewhere in the accounting records to the nominal (general) ledger.

The Banking System

12.1   A   B   This is usually the principal reason for opening a current account. If you do not wish to be able to write cheques, you should normally open a deposit account or savings account.

          C   Some banks pay interest on money in current accounts while others do not.

12.2   A   B   A bank account on which cheques can be drawn is known as a current account.

          C   Interest is paid by banks on money in deposit accounts. Interest is sometimes paid (and sometimes not) on money in current accounts, depending on which bank the account is with.

12.3   C   A   The form which must be completed when lodging money into a bank account is known as a paying-in slip or a lodgement slip.

          B   Cheques may be 'crossed' or 'uncrossed' - this is a matter for the person writing the cheque (the drawer) to decide.

12.4   C   A   Whether a cheque is 'crossed' or not has no effect on when it can be 'cashed'.

          B   The most common reason for crossing a cheque is to ensure that cheques are lodged directly into the recipient's bank account.

12.5	C	A Making a cheque void is known as 'cancelling' it.
		B Exchanging a cheque for cash at a bank is known as 'cashing' the cheque.
12.6	B	A a once-off instruction to a bank to pay a specified amount of money from your current account is a cheque.
		C a cheque is an instruction to a bank to pay a specified amount from your current account.
12.7	C	A This is the bank on which the cheque is drawn.
		B The person to whom the cheque is written is known as the 'payee'.
12.8	B	A This is the bank on which the cheque is drawn.
		C The person who writes the cheque or on whose account the cheque is written is known as the 'drawer' of the cheque.
12.9	C	A A bank overdraft is a liability.
		B A bank overdraft cannot exist on a deposit account.

Cash Books

13.1	B	Lodging cash on hand increases the bank balance (thus requiring a debit entry to increase the asset of bank) and reduces the cash balance (thus requiring a credit entry to decrease the asset of cash).
13.2	C	A credit balance brought down on the cash columns of a firm's cash book would indicate that the firm has a negative amount of cash. As this is clearly not possible, a mistake must have been made.
13.3	A	B Cash paid out cannot exceed cash received.
		C The total of cash paid out could be £100 but only if the total of cash received was £200.
		D The total of cash received could be £100 but only if there was no cash paid out.
13.4	A	B Cash discount allowed to a customer means that the customer is entitled to pay less than the full amount he owes once payment is made within an agreed time period. Payment may be made in any form, for example cash, cheque or credit transfer.
		C As for answer B above.
		D A cash discount is a reduction in the sum to be paid once payment is made within an agreed period. Obviously, if purchases are made for cash, that is, paid for immediately, payment is made on time. However, purchase invoices, arising from credit purchases, may also be paid on time.
13.5	C	A Any amount of discount deducted from the amount payable by debtors when money is received from them is cash discount allowed.
		B Discount given by a firm to its customers at the time of sale is trade discount. Cash discount is allowed at the time of payment.
13.6	A	B The total of the discount allowed column should be posted to the discount allowed account.
		C This is the correct account but the wrong side of the account.
		D As for answer B above.

The Sales Journal and the Sales Ledger

14.1 B
- A Sales invoices are the source documents which are recorded in the sales journal.
- C The sales ledger is the section of the accounting records where the accounts for individual debtors are maintained.

14.2 C
- A Money received from debtors is initially recorded is the cash book (or cash receipts book).
- B The names, addresses, credit terms and other details regarding debtors will be kept on file somewhere but not in the sales daybook.

14.3 A
- The total of the Sales Journal is the total of the credit sales for a particular period.
- B Sales are always recorded as a credit in the sales account.
- C The sales daybook is the same as the sales journal.

The Purchases Journal and the Purchases Ledger

15.1 A
- B Invoices issued to customers are recorded in the sales journal.
- C Cheques issued are recorded in the cash book (or cheque payments book).
- D Customers' orders are recorded in an order book but, as they do not represent accounting transactions, they are not entered in any book of original entry.

15.2 D
- A The total of the purchase invoices recorded in the purchases journal is posted to the debit side of the purchases account in the general ledger.
- B 'Posting' means transferring totals from the books of original entry to the double-entry accounting records. The purchases daybook is not part of these records - in fact, it is the same as the purchases journal.
- C As for answer B above.

15.3 C

5 items @ £80 each	£ 400
Less 25% trade discount	- 100
	300
Less 5% cash discount (5% of the net cost of £300)	- 15
	285

The Returns Journals

16.1 C
- A Credit notes should first be entered in the returns inwards journal, the total of which is posted to the returns inwards account, not the sales account. Only sales (the total of the sales journal) should be recorded in the sales account. Sales returns (returns inwards) should not be netted off against sales in the sales account.
- B The total of credit notes issued by a firm will eventually end up in its returns inwards account - but only after being posted from the returns inwards journal.
- D It is credit notes *received* by a firm which are initially recorded in the returns outwards journal.

16.2 D
- A Invoices sent to customers are recorded in the sales journal.
- B Invoices received from suppliers are recorded in the purchases journal.
- C Credit notes sent to customers are recorded in the returns inwards journal.

16.3	B		Cost of items returned = (£20 less 20%) each = £16 each As 12 items were returned, the total cost of all of the items returned is £16 each x 12 = £192
16.4	A	B	Returns outwards (goods going back to suppliers) are the opposite of purchases (goods coming in from suppliers). As purchases are recorded as a debit in the purchases account in the double-entry accounting records, returns outwards must be recorded as a credit.
		C	Purchases returns (returns outwards) should not be offset against purchases in the purchases account, as showing the two amounts separately provides better information about what has actually happened.
		D	As per answer B above, returns outwards must be recorded as a credit and, as per answer C above, returns outwards should not be recorded in the purchases account.
16.5	A	B	Sales returns (returns inwards) should be recorded in the returns inwards account.
		C	Sales returns (returns inwards) should not be offset against sales in the sales account, as showing the two amounts separately provides better information about what has actually happened.
		D	Returns inwards (goods being sent back by customers) are the opposite of sales (goods being sent to customers). As sales are recorded as a credit in the sales account in the double-entry accounting records, returns inwards must be recorded as a debit.

The Journal

17.1	C	A	The journal is a book of original entry, from which figures are posted to the double-entry accounting system.
		B	Cash transactions are recorded in the cash book (or cash receipts book).
17.2	B	A	Cash sales should be recorded in the cash book (or cash receipts book).
		C	Goods sold on credit should be recorded in the sales journal.

The Analytical Petty Cash Book and the Imprest System

18.1	B	There will be fewer entries in the general ledger because several transactions involving petty cash will be grouped in the petty cash book and then posted, as a single total, to the general ledger.
18.2	B	By always reimbursing the amount paid out during a period, the float (imprest) will always be restored to the amount on hand at the beginning of the period.

Value Added Tax

19.1	C		'VAT' means Value Added Tax.
19.2	B	A	VAT is paid by the purchaser of goods and services on the full price, excluding VAT, of those goods and services.
		C	VAT is charged by vendors of goods and services on the full price, excluding VAT, of those goods and services.
19.3	C		The 'standard' rate of VAT varies from time to time. At the time of going to press it is 17.5%.

19.4	B	A	VAT is not an expense for a VAT-registered firm. Therefore VAT should not appear in the profit and loss account (revenues and expenses should be shown exclusive of VAT). VAT will either be owed to, or be recoverable from, the Customs and Excise Department. This will be shown in the Balance sheet.
		C	Customers pay VAT to the firms from whom they buy goods and services - they do not pay VAT directly to the Customs and Excise Department.
		D	VAT is collected by firms from their customers - but on behalf of the Customs and Excise Department - to whom it must be periodically remitted.
19.5	A		The VAT registration limits apply to any continuous twelve-month period.
		B	The only significance of a two-month period in relation to VAT is that this is the period for which most businesses make a VAT return.
		C	31 December, although the end of many firm's accounting period, has no particular significance in relation to VAT for many businesses.
		D	As for answer B above.
19.6	B	A	As product X is zero-rated VAT is not payable on sales of this product.
		C	This would be the case if product X was exempt from VAT, not zero-rated.
19.7	D	A	The firm will be charged VAT on the purchase of goods, services and other items which are not exempt or zero-rated.
		B	The firm will be charged VAT on the purchase of services which are not exempt or zero-rated.
		C	Firms selling goods which are exempt from VAT cannot reclaim VAT paid by them on purchases.
19.8	B	A	There is no such thing as output credits - tax payable on supplies / sales is known as output tax.
		C	Irrecoverable VAT is VAT paid which cannot be reclaimed. VAT paid by a taxable person on the purchase of goods and / or services, other than goods or services in respect of which VAT cannot be reclaimed, from another taxable person would be recoverable.

19.9	B	Let Sales (excl. VAT) = 100% Therefore, Sales (incl. VAT) = 110% = £1,800 Therefore, Sales excl. VAT (100%) = £1,800 / 110 * 100 = £1,636 Proof: £1,636 + 10% = £1,800 For exam purposes, you may find it quicker, and more foolproof, to do this question as follows: Sales excluding VAT + 10% = £1,800 A £1,620 + 10% = £1,782 ; incorrect B £1,636 + 10% = £1,800 ; correct C £1,720 + 10% = £1,892 ; incorrect
19.10	B	Let Cost = 100% Cost + 21% = 121% = £200 VAT = 21% = £200 / 121 * 21 = £34.71 Proof: £200 - £34.71 = £165.29 and £165.29 + 21% = £200

| 19.11 | C | Sales incl. VAT = £11,000
VAT on sales = £11,000 / 110 * 10 = £1,000

Purchases incl. VAT = £5,500 (for re-sale) + £1,100 (other purchases) = £6,600
VAT on purchases = £6,600 / 110 * 10 = £600

VAT liability = VAT on sales - VAT on purchases = £1,000 - £600 = £400

Alternatively, this may be solved as follows:
Value added (incl. VAT) = £11,000 - £6,600 = £4,400
VAT incl. in Value added (incl. VAT) = £4,400 / 110 * 10 = £400 |
|---|---|---|
| 19.12 | A | Net sale incl. VAT = £15,000 - £6,500 =   £ 8,500.00
Net sale excl. VAT = £8,500 / 121 * 100 =   7,024.79
VAT on net sale = £7,024.79 * 21% =   1,475.21 |
| 19.13 | A | B The sales figure shown in the profit and loss account should be the total of cash sales and credit sales exclusive of VAT.
C As for answer B above. |
| 19.14 | B | A The only irrecoverable VAT which should be shown as an expense in the profit and loss account for a period is irrecoverable VAT relating to expenses incurred during that period.
C Irrecoverable VAT cannot be offset against any VAT payable on sales. |
19.15	B	In cases where VAT is recoverable, expenses should be shown in the profit and loss account net of VAT. Therefore, the amount of the expense which should be shown in this case is £12,500 / 125 * 100 = £10,000. (£10,000 + 25% = £12,500).
19.16	B	All cash / cheque payments, irrespective of what the payment relates to, are initially recorded in the cash book (or cheque payments book).
19.17	C	Fixed assets should be shown in the balance sheet net of recoverable VAT. Debtors and creditors are always shown inclusive of VAT. There must be a debit entry in the VAT account to reflect the fact that there is VAT recoverable from the Customs and Excise Department.
19.18	C	A An unregistered firm would not have a VAT account in its ledger.
B A firm dealing exclusively in goods and / or services which are exempt from VAT would not have a VAT account in its ledger.
19.19	D	A A debit balance on any nominal (general) ledger account can represent only either an asset or an expense. If VAT incurred was an expense, for example, in the case of an unregistered firm or a firm dealing exclusively in goods and / or services which are exempt from VAT, the amount of such expense would not be entered in the VAT account.
B A debit balance brought down cannot represent a liability.
C As for answer A above.
19.20	A	VAT on sales = £72,000 / 120 * 20 = £12,000
VAT on purchases = £48,000 / 120 * 20 = £8,000

VAT

Creditors	8,000	Balance b/d	2,000
Bank	3,000	Debtors	12,000
Balance c/d	*3,000*		
	14,000		14,000

19.21 C | This form is normally completed and returned every two months.

Columnar Day Books

20.1 C | A A VAT registered business should have analysis columns for VAT in all of its daybooks so that it can keep track of how much VAT it owes.

B A business which buys only zero-rated goods and services and sells goods which are liable to VAT should have an analysis column for VAT in its sales analysis book so that it can keep track of how much VAT it owes. It need not have such a column in its other daybooks.

Employees' Pay

21.1 A | Taxable pay = Gross pay - Tax Free Allowance = £24,000 - £8,000 = £16,000
Tax (PAYE) = £16,000 * 48% = £7,680.

21.2 B | A PAYE deducted from employees and not yet remitted to the Inland Revenue must also be shown as a liability in the balance sheet.

C The expense to be shown in the profit and loss account is the gross pay plus the employer's share of National Insurance Contributions.

21.3 C | A PAYE is not an expense to an employer. It is collected by employers and remitted to the Inland Revenue.

B The balance on the PAYE account at the end of a period would represent the amount of PAYE paid during the period only if there was no opening balance on the account and no wages / salaries were paid to employees during the period.

21.4 A | The PAYE / National Insurance return for any one-month taxable period (from the 6th day of one month until the 5th day of the following month) is due to be made by the 14th day of the month in which the taxable period finishes.

B It is VAT returns (Form VAT 100) which are due by the 19th day of the month following the end of a taxable period.

C It is the year-end PAYE / National Insurance return which is due by April 30 for the tax year ended 5 April.

21.5 C | A It is monthly PAYE / National Insurance returns which are due no later than the 14th day of the month in which the related taxable period finishes.

B It is VAT returns (Form VAT 100) which are due by the 19th day of the month following the end of the related taxable period.

Computers and Accounting

22.1 B | No explanation necessary.

22.2 B | No explanation necessary.

22.3 A | No explanation necessary.

Depreciation of Fixed Assets: Nature and Calculations

23.1	B	A	Charging depreciation, of itself, does not necessarily mean that funds are set aside to provide for the eventual replacement of fixed assets.
		C	The cost of fixed assets may be written off in ways other than evenly over their estimated useful economic lives.
		D	The cost of fixed assets may be written off in ways other than in ever decreasing amounts over their estimated useful economic lives.
23.2	A	B	Charging depreciation, of itself, does not necessarily mean that funds will be available for the eventual replacement of fixed assets.
		C	Cost less depreciation is unlikely to equal market value.
		D	It is the accruals concept, not the prudence concept, which underlies the charging of depreciation as an expense in the profit and loss account.
23.3	A		If the depreciation charge was capital expenditure it would be shown as an increase in fixed assets in the balance sheet - not as an expense in the profit and loss account.
23.4	A		The depreciation charge shown in the profit and loss account is an estimate of the decline in the value of fixed assets that takes place for all sorts of reasons. Obsolescence is one of those reasons but it is not the only one. For example, wear and tear and use are two other possible reasons.
23.5	D		It may be appropriate to use different methods of depreciation for different fixed assets. For example, the reducing balance method may be chosen for cars, as they decline most in value in the early years of their life, and the straight-line method chosen for plant and equipment which is used at a constant rate and which declines in value in proportion to usage. There are also many other methods of depreciation which could be used. Although SSAP 12 does not specify that any particular method of depreciation must be used at any time, once one method is chosen for a particular fixed asset (or category of fixed asset), it should be consistently used for that asset / category.
23.6	C	A	Freehold land is not normally depreciated because it has an infinite useful economic life. Sometimes, for example if freehold land is subject to coastal erosion, it should be depreciated.
		B	As per answer A above, but also assets do not have to have a significant value to be depreciated. However, SSAPs in general, as opposed to just SSAP 12, apply only to material (significant) amounts of money.
		D	Leasehold land has to be depreciated because the lease (it is the lease, not the land, which has been paid for) has a finite life. Freehold land normally does not have to be depreciated because it has an infinite useful economic life. If a building is leased and improvements are made to it, the cost of those improvements should be depreciated over the remaining term of the lease - because once the lease expires, the improvements have no value to the firm which paid for them.

| 23.7 | B | A | This would be true in relation to straight-line depreciation but it is not true in relation to reducing balance depreciation. |

C The reverse is true i.e. answer B.

D All other things being equal, profit will be greater in the later years than in the earlier years of the life of the asset because the depreciation charge is declining over time. For example,

	Year 1	Year 2	Year 3
Sales	1,000	1,000	1,000
Cost of Sales	600	600	600
Gross Profit	400	400	400
Expenses other than depreciation	200	200	200
Depreciation (Reducing balance method)	100	75	50
Net Profit (Higher in later years)	100	125	150

| 23.8 | C | A is the asset's actual cost. |

B is the asset's replacement cost.

D is the total amount of depreciation to be charged over the life of the asset.

| 23.9 | B | Annual depreciation charge using the straight-line method of depreciation = [(cost - estimated residual value) / estimated useful economic life] = (£33,000 - £11,000) / 11 = £2,000 p.a. |

| 23.10 | B | Year 1 depreciation charge = (£500,000 - £50,000) * 20% = £90,000
Year 2 depreciation charge = [(£500,000 - £50,000) - £90,000] * 20% = £72,000 |

| 23.11 | D | £200,000 * 20% = £40,000 |

Aggregate depreciation is relevant only when calculating reducing balance depreciation, which is calculated on the basis of net book value. The depreciation charge calculated by reference to the straight-line method is always a percentage of original cost or a revalued amount, less an estimated residual value, where appropriate.

23.12	B		
		Cost in 1991	£ 10,000
		1991 depreciation charge = 10% of NBV (10% of NBV = 10% of cost in year 1)	1,000
		NBV at 31 December 1991	9,000
		1992 depreciation charge = 10% of NBV =	900
		NBV at 31 December 1992	8,100
		1993 depreciation charge = 10% of NBV =	810
		NBV at 31 December 1993	7,290
		1994 depreciation charge = 10% of NBV =	729
		NBV at 31 December 1994	6,561
		1995 depreciation charge = 10% of NBV =	£656

23.13   C   1 January 1996 to 31 December 2003 = 8 years = the estimated useful life of the asset.

The total depreciation to be charged over the estimated useful life of *any* fixed asset (irrespective of depreciation method used) = Cost - Estimated scrap value = £29,800 - £5,000 = £24,800

Therefore, the total depreciation charged on this asset up to 31 December 2003 is £24,800.

You will get the same answer if you work out the depreciation year by year. If you did your solution the long way, you can check your answer against the following:

	Calculation	*Depreciation*
Cost	£ 29,800	
Depreciation Year 1 = 20% =	- 5,960	£ 5,960
	23,840	
Depreciation Year 2 = 20% =	- 4,768	4,768
	19,072	
Depreciation Year 3 = 20% =	- 3,814	3,814
	15,258	
Depreciation Year 4 = 20% =	- 3,052	3,052
	12,206	
Depreciation Year 5 = 20% =	- 2,441	2,441
	9,765	
Depreciation Year 6 = 20% =	- 1,953	1,953
	7,812	
Depreciation Year 7 = 20% =	- 1,562	1,562
	6,250	
Depreciation Year 8 = 20% =	- 1,250	1,250
	5,000	24,800

23.14   A   *Machine 1*
Cost £ 10,000
1993 Depreciation (£10,000 @ 10%) - 1,000
NBV at 31 December 1993 9,000
1994 Depreciation (£9,000 @ 10%) - 900
NBV at 31 December 1994 8,100
1995 Depreciation (£8,100 @ 10%) - 810
NBV at 31 December 1995 7,290
1996 Depreciation (£7,290 @ 10%) 729

Machine 2
Cost 8,000.00
1993 Depreciation = (£8,000 * 10% * 6/12) - 400.00
NBV at 31 December 1993 7,600.00
1994 Depreciation = (£7,600 * 10%) - 760.00
NBV at 31 December 1994 6,840.00
1995 Depreciation = (£6,840 * 10%) - 684.00
NBV at 31 December 1995 6,156.00
1996 Depreciation = (£6,156 * 10%) 615.60

Machine 3
Cost 14,000
1995 Depreciation = £14,000 * 10% * 9 months / 12 months = - 1,050
NBV at 31 December 1995 12,950
1996 Depreciation = £12,950 * 10% = - 1,295

Total depreciation charge (on all three machines) for 1996

Machine 1 (£729.00) + Machine 2 (£615.60) + Machine 3 (£1,295.00) = £2,639.60

23.15	B	Depreciation charge for year 1 = £3,200 * 25% = £800
		Depreciation charge for year 2 = (£3,200 - £800) * 25% = £600
		Total depreciation at the end of two years = £800 (year 1) + £600 (year 2) = £1,400
		NBV = Cost (£3,200) - Total depreciation (£1,400) = £1,800
23.16	C	Consider depreciation as a percentage of cost. Let cost = 100%. Depreciation, therefore, is as follows:

Year 1 = 25% of 100 =   25.0000%
Year 2 = 25% of (100 - 25) =   18.7500%
Year 3 = 25% of (100 - 25 - 18.75) =   14.0625%
                                                   57.8125%

Aggregate depreciation at the end of 3 years (57.8125% of cost) = £23,125
Therefore, 100% (cost) = (£23,125 / 57.8125) * 100 = £40,000

NBV = Cost - Aggregate depreciation at the end of 3 years = £40,000 - £23,125 = £16,875 = 42.1875% (100% - 57.8125%) of £40,000

Proof	Calculation	Depreciation
Cost	£ 40,000	
Depreciation year 1 @ 25%	10,000	10,000
	30,000	
Depreciation year 2 @ 25%	7,500	7,500
	22,500	
Depreciation year 3 @ 25%	5,625	5,625
Aggregate depreciation at the end of year 3		23,125

Double-Entry Records for Depreciation

24.1	A	The result has to be to reduce net profit (requiring a debit entry in the profit and loss account) and to reduce the book value of machinery (requiring a credit entry in the provision for depreciation of machinery account).
24.2	B	The cost of any particular category of fixed asset is shown in the trial balance as a debit balance. In order that the net book value of these assets be shown in the balance sheet, as a debit, the total depreciation charged to date on that particular category of fixed assets must be netted off against the balance on the related fixed asset account. Therefore, the balance brought down on any provision for depreciation account must be a credit balance. All ledger account balances, whether debit or credit, should be included in the trial balance.
24.3	B	The balance brought down on all ledger accounts is initially listed in the trial balance. The balances so listed are then used to prepare a profit and loss account and a balance sheet. The balance listed in the trial balance for any given provision for depreciation account will be deducted from the cost / valuation of the related fixed asset in the balance sheet - but this is after the trial balance has been prepared.

24.4	C	As money has been received, the bank balance will improve. Such an increase in an asset account requires a debit entry. The vehicle disposal account is used to calculate any profit or loss arising on the disposal. Therefore, the amount of the proceeds, clearly part of the calculation, must be recorded in that account - as a credit since the entry in the bank account is a debit.
		A The disposal of a fixed asset is not a 'sale' and therefore should not be recorded in the sales account. Only sales of goods which were purchased with the intention of being re-sold should be recorded in the sales account.
		B This is the double-entry required to transfer of cost of the vehicle being disposed of out of the vehicle account and into the vehicle disposal account.
		D This is not the correct way to record any part of a fixed asset disposal.
24.5	B	The (credit) balance on the provision for depreciation of machinery account in a firm's nominal (general) ledger represents the total depreciation charged to date on machinery currently owned by the firm. When machinery is disposed of, the total depreciation charged on it must be removed from the account - by debiting it.
		The machinery disposal account is used to calculate any profit or loss arising on the disposal of machinery. This profit or loss is calculated as the difference between the proceeds of the disposal and the net book value of the item(s) disposed of. To achieve this, both the proceeds and the net book value are transferred into the disposal account and any difference is transferred to the profit and loss account. As the net book value of a fixed asset is its cost (or valuation) less the total depreciation charged on it, both of these must be transferred into the disposal account. In the case of the total depreciation, this is achieved by answer B.
24.6	B	All profits and losses are recorded in the profit and loss account. Losses are recorded as debits and profits are recorded as credits. The profit earned or loss incurred on a disposal is 'calculated' in the relevant disposal account. In the case of a loss, the balance on this account will be a credit. This is then transferred to the profit and loss account as a debit.
24.7	B	*Period* *Calculation* *Total* 1 January - 30 April £5,000 * 10% * 4/12 £166.66 1 May - 31 August (£5,000 - £750) * 10% * 4/12 £141.66 1 September - 31 December (£5,000 - £750 + £3,000) * 10% * 4/12 £241.66 Total for the year (to the nearest pound) £550.00
24.8	C	Annual depreciation charge = (£6,000 + £260) / 5 = £1,252 Total depreciation charged = 3 years * £1,252 p.a. = £3,756 (1996 = 0) NBV = Capital cost - Total depreciation = £6,260 - £3,756 = £2,504 Profit or loss on sale = Proceeds - NBV = £5,000 - £2,504 = £2,496 Profit
24.9	A	Annual depreciation charge = (£44,000 - £2,000) / 7 = £6,000 Total depreciation charged = 4 years * £6,000 p.a. = £24,000 (1996 = 0) NBV = Cost - Total depreciation = £44,000 - £24,000 = £20,000 Profit or loss on sale = Proceeds - NBV = £18,000 - £20,000 = £2,000 loss
24.10	C	Initial annual depreciation = (£10,000 - £0) / 10 = £1,000 p.a. Aggregate depreciation to 31 December 1994 = £1,000 p.a. * 2 years = £2,000 Net Book Value (NBV) at 1 January 1995 = £10,000 - £2,000 = £8,000 Revised annual depreciation = £8,000 / 5 = £1,600 p.a.
24.11	D	Initial annual depreciation = (£4,200 - £0) / 7 = £600 p.a. Depreciation from 1 January 1993 to 31 December 1994 (2 years) = £600 * 2 = £1,200 Net Book Value (NBV) at 1 January 1995 = £4,200 - £1,200 = £3,000 Revised annual depreciation = (£3,000 - £300) / 3 = £900 p.a.

| 24.12 | B | Initial depreciation charge = (£420,000 - £20,000) / 5 = £80,000 p.a.
Depreciation charge for the years ended 31 March 1992 - 31 March 1995 (4 years) = £80,000 * 4 = £320,000
Net Book Value at 1 April 1995 before refurbishment = £420k - £320k = £100,000
Revised annual depreciation = (£100k + £240k - £60k) / 4 = £70,000 |

Capital and Revenue Expenditure

| 25.1 | C | A | If the expenditure does not have any improvement value, it is revenue expenditure and should be shown as an expense in the profit and loss account. Otherwise, it should be shown as a fixed asset in the balance sheet. |
| | | B | If there is doubt as to whether the expenditure can be recovered in future accounting periods then it must be charged as an expense in the profit and loss account (as only assets which provide benefits over a number of years are fixed assets). |

| 25.2 | C | A | is capital (not capital expenditure). |
| | | B | is revenue expenditure. |

25.3	D	A	The cost of repairing a vehicle is revenue expenditure.
		B	The cost of acquiring a vehicle for re-sale (a purchase) is revenue expenditure.
		C	Proceeds arising from the sale of a van which had been used in the business to make deliveries to customers is a capital receipt.

25.4	C	A	The annual cost of a computer maintenance contract is revenue expenditure.
		B	Legal fees relating to employee accident claims is revenue expenditure.
		D	The purchase of vehicles for re-sale is revenue expenditure

25.5	C	A	The cost of acquiring machinery for continuing use in the business is capital expenditure.
		B	The introduction of additional capital by a proprietor is capital (not capital expenditure).
		D	The transfer of surplus funds from a bank current account to a bank deposit account is not expenditure at all.

| 25.6 | C | A | The proceeds of the sale of plant and equipment is a capital receipt. |
| | | B | Money received from an insurance company as a result of crashing a delivery vehicle is a capital receipt |

25.7	D	A	the total of current assets will not be affected.
		B	the total of current liabilities will not be affected.
		C	the total of motor expenses will be overstated.

Bad Debts, Provisions for Bad Debts, Provisions for Discounts on Debtors

| 26.1 | C | A provision for bad debts is calculated by reference to the current level of debtors. These debtors have arisen (at least principally) because of sales in the current accounting period. The total of these sales is included as revenue in the profit and loss account. However, as all of these debtors may not pay, this amount of revenue is overstated. It is therefore appropriate to offset this in part by a charge to the profit and loss account. |

26.2   C   The amount of any provision for bad or doubtful debts is deducted from the debtors total which is shown as a current asset in the balance sheet. Because it is deducted, it reduces the total of current assets (relative to what the total would be if the provision was not deducted).

   A   The existence of a provision for bad or doubtful debts does not affect current liabilities.

   B   The existence of a provision for bad or doubtful debts does not affect the cost of sales.

26.3   C   The normal balance on a debtor's account - when the debtor owes money to the firm - is a debit balance. Therefore, the opposite - a credit balance - implies that the firm owes money to the debtor.

   A   If the amount owed by Murphy is considered to be a bad debt it should be written off in full, leaving a zero balance on his account. If the bad debt has not yet been written off, there would be a debit balance on Mr. Murphy's account.

   B   One or more of Murphy's cheques may have 'bounced' but this, on its own, would not cause there to be a credit balance on Murphy's account. The recording of a 'bounced' cheque from Mr. Murphy would increase the balance on his account relative to what it was before the bounced cheque was recorded. Although this could leave a credit balance on his account (if there was a higher credit balance on the account before the dishonoured cheque was recorded) this would not be normal and certainly the existence of a credit balance on a debtor's account does not indicate that a cheque from a debtor has been dishonoured.

   D   The normal balance on a debtor's account - when the debtor owes money to the firm - is a debit balance. Therefore, the opposite - a credit balance - implies that the firm owes money to the debtor. There is therefore no possibility of not being paid the present balance. Consequently, there is no need to make a provision against this account.

26.4   B   The purpose of the bad debts account is to accumulate the total of the bad debts written off during an accounting period. As writing off bad debts is an expense, this total must then be charged in the profit and loss account.

   In general, the difference between the two sides of an expense or revenue account is transferred to the profit and loss account - a balance is not carried down (and therefore not brought down) on these types of accounts. On the other hand, the difference between the two sides of an asset or liability account (balance sheet accounts) is the balance on that account - to be listed in the trial balance and subsequently shown in the balance sheet.

26.5   D   Cash discount (also known as settlement discount) is allowed only to those customers who pay their accounts on time. The total amount of debtors estimated to pay their accounts on time equals total debtors less bad debts (these customers already owe money for some time) less the provision for bad debts (an estimate of the amount currently owed by debtors which it is probable will never be received - let alone received in time to warrant a cash discount).

Other Adjustments for Final Accounts

27.1   D   Current liabilities are amounts payable which are due to be discharged within one year. Accruals, being amounts owing in respect of expenses, are normally due to be paid within one year. Therefore, accruals should be shown as part of current liabilities.

27.2   D   Prepayments are amounts paid in advance in respect of expenses. As this means that the benefit of the money paid is yet to be received, prepayments are clearly an asset (a resource). As the advance payment normally covers no longer than the next 12 months, this asset is a current asset.

27.3   A   A trial balance is a list of the balances brought down in the underlying ledger accounts. In a trial balance, credit balances represent income or liabilities whereas debit balances represent assets or expenses. In the case of rent payable, a credit balance represents a liability as rent payable cannot be income.

27.4	A	Accruals, being amounts due, are a liability. As they are amounts due in respect of expenses, they must be shown as expenses in the profit and loss account.
		B Expenses should clearly not be shown as income in the profit and loss account and amounts due but unpaid should clearly be shown as a liability in the balance sheet.
		C Expenses due but unpaid are likely to be payable within a year of the balance sheet date. They should therefore be shown as current liabilities, not long-term liabilities (amounts payable after more than one year from the balance sheet date).
		D Assets (prepayments) and liabilities (accruals) should always be shown separately in the balance sheet rather than being netted off against each other as this provides better (more complete) information.
27.5	D	Prepayments, being money paid for benefits yet to be received, are assets. As they are amounts paid in respect of future accounting periods, the expense to be shown in the profit and loss account for a period will be less than the amount paid during that period, by the amount of the prepayment (an application of the accruals concept).
27.6	C	Any expense paid in advance is a prepayment. In accordance with the accruals concept, the amount to be shown in the profit and loss account in relation to any expense is the amount of the expense relevant to that period. In this case, the relevant amount is less than the amount paid, by the amount of the prepayment.
27.7	B	A The accounting concept which gives rise to adjustments at the end of an accounting period in respect of accruals and prepayments is the accruals concept.
		C Revenue should be shown in the profit and loss account even when the associated payment has not been received so long as the revenue relates to the current accounting period and payment is likely to be received. For example, credit sales, where payment has not yet been received are included in the profit and loss account as well as cash sales, where payment has been received. The amount not yet received is shown as debtors in the balance sheet.
27.8	C	For example, if, before any accrual or prepayment adjustments were made, net profit was £2,000 then, by accruing £500 in respect of wages, net profit would be £1,500 whereas by recording a prepayment of £500 in respect of wages net profit would be £2,500 - a difference of £1,000 (overstated).
27.9	A	The figure shown in the preliminary trial balance is the balance on the rent account before any adjustments are made in respect of accruals or prepayments at the end of the accounting period. This consists of any opening balance plus the payments made prior to the date of the preliminary trial balance. As this firm is new, there is no opening balance. Therefore, the figure in the trial balance will be £0 + three payments of £2,500 each = £7,500.
27.10	B	In accordance with the accruals concept, the income figure to be shown in the profit and loss account is the income earned during the period covered by the profit and loss account, irrespective of whether received or not = £10,000 * 10% = £1,000.
27.11	B	£1,320 = 1994 expense + 10%. Therefore, 1994 expense = (£1,320 / 110 * 100) = £1,200. Only half of the 1994 expense (£600) was paid in 1994. Therefore, the other half (£600) was due at 1 January 1995. As there is no accrual or prepayment at 31 December 1995, the £1,320 paid has to be made up of the £600 in respect of 1994 and the balance - £720 - in respect of the full expense for 1995.

27.12	A					
				Rent		
		Bank	£12,750	Balance b/d		£2,500
				Profit and Loss		*£9,000*
				Balance c/d (£3,750 / 3 prepaid)		£1,250
			£12,750			£12,750

27.13 B Year-end Prepayment
Policy X = January to June 1996 = 6 months @ £240 p.a. =   £120
Policy Y = January to April 1996 = 4 months @ £1,200 p.a. = £400
   Total =   £520

			Insurance		
	Bank	3,000	*Profit and Loss*		2,480
			Balance c/d (above)		520
		£3,000			£3,000

27.14 C For example, if the rent receivable applicable to the year is £100 and £175 has been received, then, in accordance with the accruals concept, the amount to be shown in the profit and loss account is £100, £75 less than the amount received. This would be shown as follows:

		Rent Receivable		
Profit and Loss	100	Bank		175
Balance c/d	75			
	£175			£175

27.15 B

		Rent & Rates		
Balance b/d (Rates prepaid)	600	Balance b/d (Rent accrued)		900
Bank (Rent paid)	4,800	*Profit and Loss*		*8,000*
Bank (Rates paid)	3,100			
Balance c/d (Rent accrued)	1,100	Balance c/d (Rates prepaid)		700
	£9,600			£9,600

27.16 A

		Rent & Rates		
Balance b/d (Rates prepaid)	3,000	Balance b/d (Rent accrued)		2,500
Bank	34,500	Profit & Loss (Expense for the year)		36,000
Balance c/d (Rent due)	4,500	Balance c/d (Rates prepaid)		3,500
	£42,000			£42,000

27.17 A In any ledger account, a debit balance brought down represents either an asset or an expense and a credit balance brought down represents either a liability or income. Since the balance on an expense account is either an accrual or a prepayment, the £50 balance has to be a prepayment (asset) and the £100 balance has to be an accrual (liability). This rules out options B (£100 asset), C (£100 asset) and D (£50 liability). When the stationery expense is prepaid, there is a stock of stationery remaining at the end of the year.

The Valuation of Stock

28.1 D As per SSAP 9.

28.2 A Stock should be valued at the lower of its cost and its net realisable value (NRV) on an item-by-item or category-by-category basis (not on a total basis)

Category	*Cost*	*NRV*	*Lower of Cost and NRV*
1	£ 35,000	£ 22,000	£ 22,000
2	22,000	25,000	22,000
			44,000

28.3	C	As per SSAP 9.
28.4	A	The net realisable value of an item of stock is its actual or estimated selling price less all further costs to completion and all costs to be incurred in marketing, selling and distributing the item. In this case, this is £1,600 - £110 - £130 = £1,360. According to SSAP9, when the NRV of an item is less than its cost, the item should be valued at its NRV, i.e. £1,360.
28.5	C	The prudence concept means that profit should not be anticipated and all foreseeable losses should be provided for as soon as they are foreseen. If stock was valued at an amount greater than its cost (NRV usually is greater than cost) it would include an element of profit, which, as the stock is not yet sold, would be an anticipation of profit. If stock was valued at its cost, when its net realisable value was lower, this would not be anticipating a foreseeable loss.
28.6	C	The abbreviation 'FIFO' means the First-In-First-Out method of approximating the cost of stock.
28.7	C	The abbreviation 'LIFO' means the Last-In-First-Out method of approximating the cost of stock.
28.8	B	The last in, first out (LIFO) method is not normally acceptable because, if it is used, the resulting approximation of cost will not approximate recent costs. These recent costs should be reflected because it is normal to sell the oldest stock items first, thus leaving the newer ones (at the most recent costs) in stock.
28.9	A	The oldest stock costs are those incurred in buying stock some time ago. Assuming that these items of stock are now deemed to have been sold (as is the case with the First-In-First-Out method) their cost will not have an effect on the closing stock valuation as only the more recent purchases are deemed to remain in stock under this method.
28.10	B	Under the LIFO method, as the most recent items purchased are deemed to be sold before items previously purchased, the cost of these new items (the lowest costs, as prices are falling) will be matched against sales, thus leaving the first items purchased (the higher costs, as prices are falling) remaining in stock.
28.11	B	Under the LIFO method, the most-recent stock items purchased are deemed to be sold before those purchased previously. Profit is calculated as the excess of the revenue from the sale of the items over their deemed cost, thereby matching revenues with up-to-date costs.
28.12	B	Although the LIFO method yields a cost of sales figure which most accurately reflects the actual cost of sales under normal circumstances its use is not permitted when preparing financial statements for publication.
28.13	B	The consistency concept means that similar items should be accounted for in a similar way from one accounting period to the next. Therefore, stock should be valued consistently over time. This would not be the case if the method used to value it, or approximate its cost, changed from year to year.

28.14 A For example, if stock at 1 January and stock at 31 December were both originally valued at £10,000, sales were £100,000, purchases were £50,000 and expenses were £30,000 then the situation would be as follows.

	Originally Reported		Revised after correcting stock errors	
Sales		100,000		100,000
Stock at 1 January	10,000		12,000	
Purchases	50,000		50,000	
Stock at 31 December	- 10,000		- 7,000	
Cost of Sales		- 50,000		- 55,000
Gross Profit		50,000		45,000
Expenses		- 30,000		- 30,000
Net Profit		20,000		15,000

Bank Reconciliation Statements

29.1 C A A statement sent by banks to their customers is a 'bank statement' - i.e. a statement showing details of all transactions recorded by the bank on the customers' accounts and the balances on those accounts.

B Banks do send letters to customers who exceed their agreed credit limit with the bank but these letters are not known as bank reconciliation statements.

29.2 D A A projection of the firm's future cash inflows and outflows is required to ascertain the amount of financing, if any, which it may require in the future.

B A calculation, not a reconciliation, is required to ascertain whether bank charges have been correctly calculated by the bank.

C A calculation, not a reconciliation, is required to ascertain whether the correct amount of interest has been paid to the firm by the bank on all money on deposit.

29.3 B A bank reconciliation statement is a reconciliation between a figure in the nominal (general) ledger (double-entry records) and a figure on a bank statement. It is prepared at the end of an accounting period after all double-entry records for that period have been completed.

29.4 D A a standing order is an instruction to a bank to pay a specified amount out of one's account at regular intervals.

B a dishonoured cheque is a cheque returned by a bank to the person who presented it because there are insufficient funds in the drawer's account to meet the cheque.

C a credit transfer is a transfer of funds from a person or bank account into another bank account.

29.5 C A This balance may be incorrect (may not be the true amount of money available to the firm) because it does not take account of, for example, cheques written but not yet cashed.

B This balance may be incorrect (may not be the true amount of money available to the firm) because it does not take account of bank charges, standing orders, dishonoured cheques, direct debits, credit transfers and other items shown on the bank statement.

29.6	A	These cheques (outstanding cheques) must be included in the bank reconciliation statement because they will have been recorded in the accounting records but have not been recorded in the bank statement. They therefore give rise to a difference between the two balances.
	B	Accruals are amounts unpaid at the balance sheet date - not amounts that have been paid by cheque.
	C	Cheques should be cancelled by the drawer (the person who wrote them) when he / she does not wish them to be cashed.
	D	A 'stale' cheque is one which is dated more than six months ago and therefore cannot be cashed.
29.7	D	A Errors made by the bank will give rise to a difference because the same errors will not have been made in the nominal (general) ledger.
		B Cheques written by the firm which have not yet appeared on its bank statement (outstanding cheques) will give rise to a difference because they have been recorded as having been issued in the nominal (general) ledger but they are not recorded in the bank statement.
		C Lodgements made by the firm which have not yet appeared on its bank statement (outstanding lodgements) will give rise to a difference because they have been recorded in the nominal (general) ledger but they are not recorded in the bank statement.
29.8	C	Once the cheques are written, the money is no longer available to the firm. However, according to the bank statement, this money is still available as it is not yet recorded on the bank statement.

29.9   D

Correction of Ledger

Bank

Balance c/d	4,100	Balance b/d	3,600
		Dishonoured cheque	500
	4,100		4,100

Bank Reconciliation Statement as at 31 March

Balance per ledger (corrected)	- 4,100
Outstanding lodgements	- 2,000
Cheques not presented	1,400
Balance per bank statement	- 4,700

29.10   A

Computation of Correct Ledger Balance as at 31 December

Balance per the bank statement	- 1,000
Outstanding lodgements	5,000
Cheques not presented	- 3,000
Correct balance per the ledger (debit)	1,000

However, as the dishonoured cheque has not yet been entered in the ledger, the actual ledger balance exceeds the correct ledger balance by £500. Therefore, the actual ledger balance is £500 debit.

29.11   C

Balance per John Smith's ledger	£1,518
Invoice not yet recorded in the ledger	520
Amount owed by John Smith to Alpha Ltd.	2,038
Cheque paid to Alpha Ltd. not yet recorded by Alpha Ltd.	- 250
Balance shown on statement from Alpha Ltd.	1,788

Control Accounts

30.1 B — The twin effects of receiving money from debtors are that the bank balance will be increased when the money is lodged and the debtors owe less than they previously did. To increase an asset account (bank), that account must be debited (therefore, debit the bank account) and to decrease an asset account (debtors), that account must be credited (therefore credit the debtors control account).

30.2 C — Debtors becoming bad debts means that less will now be collected from them than would otherwise have been the case. Therefore, the value of debtors (an asset) has been reduced. A credit entry is required to record a decrease in an asset account.

30.3 D — The primary purpose of a debtors control account is to act as a 'control' over the debtors (sales) ledger. The control mechanism is to compare the sum of the balances on the individual debtors accounts with the balance on the debtors control account.

30.4 C — The primary purpose of a creditors control account is to act as a 'control' over the creditors ledger. The control mechanism is to compare the sum of the balances on the individual creditors accounts with the balance on the creditors control account.

30.5 C — Returns outwards (purchases returns) should be recorded in the creditors control account.

    A A credit note being issued to a debtor immediately after he had paid his account in full would result in a credit balance on that debtor's account and therefore, possibly, a credit balance on the debtors control account.

    B A debtor paying more than the amount owed by him on his account would result in a credit balance on that debtor's account and therefore, possibly, a credit balance on the debtors control account.

    D Discount allowed being recorded twice in the debtors control account could, if the amount was large enough relative to the amount owed by debtors, result in a credit balance on the debtors control account.

30.6 D — Based solely on the total of the credit sales (£230,000) and the total amount received from debtors (£190,000) it would appear that debtors increased by £40,000. However, the actual increase is £50,000. Therefore, the correct solution is the one which, when corrected, would increase the balance on the debtors control account.

    A Recording discount allowed not previously recorded would reduce the balance on the debtors control account.

    B Recording bad debts not previously recorded would reduce the balance on the debtors control account.

    C Recording sales returns not previously recorded would reduce the balance on the debtors control account.

30.7 B

Creditors

Bank	94,000	Balance b/d	15,000
Balance c/d	8,000	Purchases	87,000
	102,000		102,000

30.8 C

Debtors

Balance b/d	900	Bank	5,000
		Bad Debts	100
Sales (Credit)	5,700	Balance c/d	1,500
	6,600		6,600

30.9	C	Credit purchases = £950,000 * 80% = £760,000. Assume that creditors owed £20,000 at the beginning of the year and did not owe anything at the end of the year (a reduction of £20,000 over the course of the period).

Creditors

Bank	780,000	Balance b/d	20,000
Balance c/d	0	Purchases	760,000
	780,000		780,000

30.10	B	*Debtors*

Balance b/d	11,500	Bank	45,000
Sales	48,000	Balance c/d	14,500
	59,500		59,500

30.11	C	*Creditors*

Bank	32,000	Balance b/d	2,500
Balance c/d	4,200	Purchases	33,700
	36,200		36,200

30.12	D	*Creditors*

Discount Received	1,000	Balance b/d	4,600
Returns Outwards	6,000	Purchases	54,000
Bank	39,000	Bank	2,000
Debtors	1,000		
Balance c/d	13,600		
	60,600		60,600

30.13	B	£1,000 - £50 = £950. The provision for bad debts is never entered in the control account.
30.14	C	The original £6,000 balance is net of the £300 bad debt. The provision for bad debts is not relevant to the control account. When the bad debt is recovered, the £300 originally written off is reinstated by debiting the control account and crediting the bad debts account. The entry to record the money received is to debit the bank account and credit the debtors control account.
30.15	B	Neither the provision for bad and doubtful debts or the cash sales are relevant to the debtors control account.

Debtors

Balance b/d	10,000	Bank	25,000
Sales (Credit)	30,000	Bad Debts	1,000
		Balance c/d	14,000
	40,000		40,000

30.16	B	Cash sales are not relevant to the debtors control account.

Debtors

Balance b/d	8,000	Bank	80,000
Sales (Credit)	89,000	Discount Allowed	1,000
		Returns Inwards	6,000
		Balance c/d	10,000
	97,000		97,000

30.17 B   Cash purchases are not relevant to the creditors control account.

Creditors

Discount Received	500	Balance b/d	5,000
Returns Outwards	3,500	Purchases (Credit)	60,000
Bank	54,000		
Balance c/d	*7,000*		
	65,000		65,000

30.18 C

Debtors

Balance b/d	5,000	Bank	15,000
Bad Debt Recovered	4,000	Bank (Bad Debt Recovered)	4,000
		Discount Allowed	1,000
		Bad Debts	2,000
Sales (Credit)	*19,000*	Balance c/d (£5,000 + 20%)	6,000
	28,000		28,000

30.19 C   Because of 2% discount, £147,000 received = 98% of debt owed. Therefore, discount = £147,000 / 98 * 2 = £3,000.

Debtors

Balance b/d	22,000	Bank	147,000
		Discount Allowed (Above)	3,000
		Bad Debts	3,500
Sales (Credit)	*155,500*	Balance c/d	24,000
	177,500		177,500

30.20 A   £29,175 - (£80 x 2) + (£67 x 2) - £220 - £72 = £28,857.

30.21 A   £39,150 - (£70 x 2) + (£40 x 2) - £60 = £39,030.

30.22 A   The undercasting of the list of balances does not affect the control account.

£37,564 + (£140 x 2) - (£310 x 2) - £276 = £36,948.

30.23 C   A Discounts allowed being omitted from the nominal (general) ledger but correctly accounted for in the debtors ledger would result in the balance on the debtors control account being greater than the total of the list of debtors balances.

B A credit balance on a debtors ledger account being treated as a debit balance would result in the balance on the debtors control account being greater than the total of the list of debtors balances.

Errors not Affecting Trial Balance Agreement

31.1 D   A The incorrect sales invoice will result in the total of the sales journal being incorrect. Therefore, an incorrect figure will be posted to the ledger. So long as this (incorrect) figure is posted to the correct sides of the correct accounts (the debit side of the debtors control account and the credit side of the sales account) this will be an error of original entry.

B This transaction will not be recorded because an invoice was not issued. This will therefore be an error of omission.

C Assuming that the double-entry for the (incorrect) depreciation charge is correct, this will be an error of original entry.

31.2	C	The total of expenses would be understated because the £200 motor expenses would be omitted from the list of expenses.
		A Gross profit would not be affected.
		B Net profit would be overstated.
		D Net assets would be overstated.
31.3	C	A All corrections, just like all transactions, ultimately have to be recorded in the ledger anyway.
		B As per answer A above.
		D Errors are not corrected in control accounts.

Suspense Accounts and Errors

32.1	D	Although what is described in answers A, B and C are incorrect, none of these errors affect the balancing of the trial balance. As the trial balance will balance in all cases, these errors will not be disclosed by it.
		A As the expenses are being entered in the wrong class of account (sales is an income account), this is an error of principle.
		B A £300 credit sale being entered in the Sales Journal as £30 will result in the total of the sales journal being incorrect. So long as this incorrect figure is posted to the correct sides of the correct accounts (the debit side of the debtors control account and the credit side of the sales account) this will be an error of original entry.
		C Failure to record any transaction is an error of omission.
32.2	A	The only purpose served by a suspense account is to force an unbalanced trial balance to balance by recording the amount of the imbalance in the suspense account until such time as the underlying error(s) can be located. At least initially, there is no reason to record this amount in any other account. Some or all of the amount of the imbalance may be recorded in a control account, a provision account or a liability account, but also may be recorded in other accounts, for example asset or expense accounts, once the reason(s) for the imbalance has / have been discovered.
32.3	B	A Miscellaneous expenses should be entered in a Miscellaneous Expenses account, the total of which is then transferred to the profit and loss account.
		C Bad debts recovered should be entered in a Bad Debts Recovered account, the total of which is then transferred to the profit and loss account.
32.4	D	If the underlying error(s) are not located and corrected before preparing financial statements the financial statements may be materially incorrect (they will be materially incorrect unless some of the errors discovered offset each other).
		A Including a material debit balance on a suspense account as an asset in the balance sheet may overstate assets as the reason for the debit balance on the suspense account may be unrecorded expenses.
		B Including a material debit balance on a suspense account as an expense in the profit and loss account may understate profit as the reason for the debit balance on the suspense account may be unrecorded assets.
		C A debit balance on an account cannot represent a liability. A liability has to be a credit balance. A debit balance can only be either an asset or an expense.

32.5	C	Bank charges result in the bank balance being reduced. All reductions in the bank balance are initially recorded in the Cash Book (or cheque payments book) and subsequently posted to the nominal (general) ledger.
	A	Bank charges, like all other transactions and events, should initially be recorded in a book of original entry and subsequently recorded in the general (nominal) ledger.
	B	As for answer A above.
	D	No transaction is ever initially recorded in the suspense account. A suspense account arises only after all transactions have been recorded in the nominal (general) ledger, either directly, or via the books of original entry, and a trial balance prepared which is found to be out of balance.

Introduction to Accounting Ratios

33.1	A	Gross Profit Margin = Gross Profit as a percentage of selling price = (£625 - £500) / £625 = 20%.
33.2	B	Mark-up (on cost) = Gross Profit as a percentage of cost price = (£625 - £500) / £500 = 25%.
33.3	A	Mark-up on cost = Profit as a percentage of cost price = 25% Let cost = £100 Therefore, profit = £25 Selling price = Cost + gross profit = £125 Gross profit Margin = Gross Profit as a percentage of selling price = £25 / £125 = 20%.
33.4	C	Gross Profit Margin = Gross Profit as a percentage of selling price = 20% Let selling price = £100 Therefore, gross profit = £20 Therefore, cost = £80 Mark-up on cost = Profit as a percentage of cost price £20 / £80 = 25%.
33.5	D	Cost of sales = Sales * 100 / 120 £16,000 = Sales * 100 / 120 Therefore, Sales = £16,000 * 120 / 100 = £19,200 Therefore, none of the answers given is correct.
33.6	B	Cost of sales + 33 1/3% = £240,000 Therefore, Cost of sales = £180,000 Cost of sales = Opening stock + purchases - closing stock Therefore, £180,000 = £10,300 + £186,000 - closing stock Therefore, closing stock = £16,300
33.7	A	Cost of sales + 25% = £200,000 Therefore, Cost of sales = £160,000 Cost of sales = Opening stock + purchases - closing stock Therefore, £160,000 = £50,000 + £130,000 - closing stock Therefore, closing stock = £20,000
33.8	D	Stock Turnover = Cost of Sales / Average Stock

Single Entry and Incomplete Records

34.1 A Let opening debtors = 0. Therefore, closing debtors = £40,000.

Debtors

Balance b/d	0	Bank	560,000
Sales (Credit) (£750k * 80%)	600,000	Balance c/d	40,000
	600,000		600,000

34.2 A Days credit given = (Debtors / Credit sales) * 360
Therefore, 60 = (£60,000 / Credit sales) * 360
Therefore, Credit sales = £360,000
Cost + 25% = £360,000
Therefore, Cost = £288,000
Gross profit = Sales - Cost of sales = £360,000 - £288,000 = £72,000

34.3 B Let sales in the low season = X.
Therefore, Sales in the high season = 1.5X.
Total sales = £283,500 = (9 * X) + (3 * 1.5X) = 13.5X.
Therefore X = £283,500 / 13.5 = £21,000.
Sales in 9 off-peak months = 9 * £21,000 = £189,000.
Sales in 3 summer months = 3 * £21,000 * 1.5 = £94,500.

	3 months	9 months	Total
Sales	£94,500	£189,000	£283,500
Gross Profit Margin	25%	20%	
Gross Profit (sales * gross profit margin)	£23,625	£37,800	
Cost of Sales (sales - gross profit)	£70,875	£151,200	£222,075

34.4 B Fixed Assets + Net Current Assets = Net Assets
Fixed Assets + £3,000 = £8,000
Therefore, Fixed Assets = £5,000

34.5 A Opening capital + Profit (-loss) - Drawings = Closing capital
£16,500 + profit or loss - £3,300 = £11,350
Therefore, loss = £1,850

34.6 D

Debtors

Balance b/d	4,800	Bank	127,600
		Discount Allowed	2,400
		Bad Debts	800
Sales (Credit)	131,400	Balance b/d	5,400
	136,200		136,200

Total Sales = Cash Sales + Credit Sales = £23,200 + £131,400 = £154,600

Creditors

Bank	93,200	Balance b/d	6,300
		Bank	80
Balance c/d	5,900	Purchases (Credit)	92,720
	99,100		99,100

Cost of Sales = Opening Stock + Purchases - Closing Stock
= £10,300 + £92,720 - £10,600 = £92,420

Gross profit = Sales - Cost of sales = £154,600 - £92,420 = £62,180

Receipts & Payments Accounts and Income & Expenditure Accounts

35.1	B		A receipts and payments account is a summary of cash and bank transactions for a period.
		A	A Receipts and Payments Account is prepared on a cash basis, not on an accruals basis. A Receipts and Payments Account, adjusted for accruals and prepayments, is an Income and Expenditure account.
		C	Purchases and sales are not shown in a receipts and payments account although the related receipts and payments are - as are receipts and payments in respect of many other items.
35.2	B		Monetary inflows are shown on one side of a Receipts and Payments Account and monetary outflows on the other. Therefore, the difference (the balance on the account) has to be the total of cash and bank balances.
		A	Net profit and net loss are terms confined to commercial organisations and are calculated in profit and loss accounts. Receipts and payments accounts are prepared for non-trading organisations, such as clubs. The equivalent of profits and losses for such organisations (surplus or deficit of income over expenditure) are calculated by preparing an income and expenditure account.
		C	Any excess of a club's income over its expenditure for a particular period is shown in its income and expenditure account.
		D	Any excess of a club's expenditure over its income for a particular period is shown in its income and expenditure account.
35.3	B		Even in the case of a non-trading organisation, a trading and profit and loss account should be prepared for any 'commercial' activities, and the net result transferred to the club's income and expenditure account. Profits should be shown in the income section and losses should be shown in the expenditure section.
35.4	A		A club's accumulated fund is the same as a sole trader's capital. From the accounting equation, we know that Capital = Assets - Liabilities.
35.5	A	B	is a liability.
		C	is a receipt.
35.6	B		In accordance with the accruals concept, the subscription income for the year is the amount of subscriptions relevant to the year (irrespective of whether received or not). The amount relevant to the year is 50 members @ £20 each = £1,000.

35.7 A

Subscriptions

Balance b/d (Arrears)	80	Balance b/d (Advance)	100
Income and Expenditure	1,000	*Bank*	*960*
Balance c/d (Advance)	40	Balance c/d (Arrears)	60
	1,120		1,120

35.8 C The prudence concept means that revenue or profit should not be anticipated and losses should be provided for as soon as they are foreseen. By not including subscriptions due as revenue for the year, the club is not anticipating revenue and therefore applying the prudence concept.

35.9	B	A credit balance on any account represents either income or a liability.
	A	A long-term loan to life members would be an asset and therefore a debit balance.
	C	Life subscriptions cannot be due. A person does not become a life member until they have paid their subscription.
	D	Only a fraction of the balance on the life subscriptions account is revenue for the current year - not the whole balance.

Manufacturing Accounts

36.1	A	*Item 1*	Depreciation of productive plant and machinery is shown in the manufacturing account (as an indirect factory cost (overhead)) as the machinery is located in the factory.
		Item 2	The amount of the factory supervisor's wages is shown in the manufacturing account (as an indirect factory cost (overhead)) as the supervisor works in the factory.
		Item 3	Depreciation of an office building is shown as an expense in the profit and loss account as the building is used for non-manufacturing purposes.
36.2	A	B	Work-in-progress is adjusted for in the manufacturing account.
		C	Direct material costs are included in the manufacturing account under the heading 'prime cost'.
		D	Carriage charged on raw materials purchased is included in the manufacturing account under the heading 'prime cost'.
36.3	C	A	The accruals concept is applied when preparing a manufacturing account. Therefore, costs incurred, not costs paid, is the relevant amount.
		B	Non-factory costs are not included in the manufacturing account.
		D	Gross profit is calculated in the trading and profit and loss account.
36.4	C	A	Production cost includes, but is not limited to, the cost of direct materials.
		B	Production cost includes, but is not limited to, the cost of direct materials and direct wages.
		D	Administration expenses are shown as an expense in the profit and loss account.
36.5	D		A direct expense is one that can be traced to specific units of output. Items 1, 2 and 3 can be so traced. Item 4 cannot.
36.6	A	B	The cost of lubricating oils for machinery and vehicles is an indirect cost.
		C	The factory supervisor's salary is an indirect cost.
36.7	B		Cost of Sales includes 'production cost of goods completed' which, in turn, includes all factory costs.
		A	Depreciation on the factory premises is a factory cost and, as such, would be (indirectly) included in 'cost of sales'.
		C	Carriage charged on raw materials purchased is a factory cost and, as such, would be (indirectly) included in 'cost of sales'.
36.8	B		Prime cost = the sum of the cost of *direct* materials, the cost of *direct* labour and the cost of *direct* expenses. Factory overhead expenses are an *indirect* cost.

36.9	A		Prime cost = the sum of the cost of *direct* materials, the cost of *direct* labour and the cost of *direct* expenses.
		B	The wages of factory workers wholly engaged in machine maintenance is an *indirect* cost.
		C	The depreciation of lorries used for deliveries to customers is an *indirect* cost.
		D	The cost of indirect production materials is an *indirect* cost.
36.10	A		Prime cost = the sum of the cost of direct materials, *the cost of direct labour* and the cost of direct expenses.
36.11	D		Depreciation of factory plant and equipment is clearly a factory cost so it should appear in the manufacturing account but not under the heading 'prime cost' as it is an indirect cost.
36.12	D		Accountancy fees are not a factory cost so should not appear in the manufacturing account at all. Neither are they related to selling and distribution so they should not be included in selling and distribution expenses.
36.13	C		Prime cost = the sum of *the cost of direct materials*, the cost of direct labour and the cost of direct expenses.
36.14	B		Prime cost = direct materials + direct labour + direct expenses = £250,000 + £100,000 + £12,000 = £362,000
36.15	C		Prime cost = direct materials + direct labour + direct expenses = (£750 + £1,750 + £500 - £500) + £1,000 + 0 = £3,500 Cost of sales = opening stock of finished goods + Production cost - closing stock of finished goods = £2,000 + (£3,500 + £6,200) - £1,500 = £10,200 Gross profit = Sales - Cost of sales = £20,250 - £10,200 = £10,050
36.16	D	A	The reducing balance method gives the highest figure in the first year and this figure declines thereafter.
		B	The sum-of-the-years'-digits method gives the highest figure in the first year and this figure declines thereafter.
		C	The straight-line method gives the same figure every year.

Departmental Accounts

37.1	A	B	A departmental profit and loss account may help to estimate future cash requirements but this is not the purpose of preparing it.
		C	Departmental profit and loss accounts do not ensure that all likely bad debts are provided for.
		D	Departmental profit and loss accounts do not ensure that discounts allowed do not exceed discounts received.
37.2	B		It is likely that the management of each department will be evaluated based on their department's financial results. It is clearly unfair to expect someone to be responsible for costs which are not within their control. Other bases of allocating costs are acceptable in certain circumstances where there is a relationship between expenses allocated and the basis used for the allocation.

Partnership Accounts: An Introduction

38.1 C — All that's required to form a partnership is for two or more people to agree to become business partners. They do not have to agree anything else. However, in order to avoid disputes and ill-feeling later on, it is preferable that they agree all relevant matters and record these in some kind of formal written agreement.

38.2 A
- B The creditors of the firm have no say in the matter (the partnership wouldn't have any creditors until after it has been formed anyway).
- C The Partnership Act, 1890 governs the rights and liabilities of partners among themselves only in the absence of verbal or written agreement.

38.3 A — Someone must always be responsible for the debts of the firm. This is a major disadvantage of partnerships relative to companies. However, once one person accepts this responsibility, all other partners can be limited partners.

38.4 D
- A By debiting a partner's share of profits to his / her capital account the balance on the account will decline (not remain fixed).
- B By crediting a partner's share of profits to his / her capital account the balance on the account will increase (not remain fixed).
- C By debiting a partner's share of profits to his / her current account the balance on that account will decline, indicating that the firm owes less to the partner as a result of making a profit!

38.5 C — In the absence of a partnership agreement, the main provisions of the Partnership Act, 1890 are:

That partners share profits and losses equally.

Interest on capital is not paid to partners.

Interest is not charged on partners' drawings.

Partners are not paid salaries.

Interest is paid to partners at the rate of 5% per annum on advances made by them to the partnership in excess of the capital they have agreed to contribute.

38.6 D

		John	Mary	
Profit for the year				£ 80,000
Salary		£ 14,000	£ 20,000	- 34,000
Interest on capital (10%)		4,000	6,000	- 10,000
Profit remaining				36,000
Share of profit (40% : 60%)		14,400	21,600	36,000
Totals receivable		£32,400	£47,600	£80,000

38.7 B

	Jack	Diane	
Profit for the year			£ 40,000
Salary	£ 18,000	£ 22,000	- 40,000
Interest on capital (10%)	2,000	3,000	- 5,000
Loss to be shared			- 5,000
Share of loss (40% : 60%)	- £2,000	- £3,000	- £5,000

38.8 B — Capital = Cash (£15,000) + Value of the building to the partnership (£60,000 market value - £35,000 mortgage) = £40,000

Goodwill in Partnership Accounts

39.1 C In the context of acquiring a business, goodwill is the difference between the price paid for the business as a whole and the sum of the values of the individual (net) assets. In this case, this is as follows:

Price paid for the business	£ 140,000
Values of the individual (net) assets (£50,000 + £15,000 + £5,000 + £40,000)	110,000
Goodwill	30,000

39.2 A

Current annual earnings		£ 19,500
Alternative annual earnings		
Salary	£ 11,000	
Interest (£35,000 * 6.5%)	2,275	- 13,275
Annual super-profit		6,225
5 years' purchase =		£31,125

39.3 A Goodwill = £10,500 x 3 = £31,500
Ben's original share = £31,500 x 1/3rd = £10,500
Ben's new share = £31,500 x 2/7ths = £9,000
Adjustment required = £10,500 - £9,000 = £1,500 reduction.
A credit entry is required in the capital account to compensate for this reduction in goodwill.

Partnership Accounts Continued: The Revaluation of Assets

40.1 B If assets were not revalued, a partner leaving the firm may not receive his / her full entitlements or a partner joining the firm may not be asked to bring in enough to pay for his / her share.

40.2 C Losses are always debited to the partners' capital / current accounts whereas profits are always credited to them. The retiring partner bears a share of the loss because it arose while he / she was still a partner.

An Introduction to the Final Accounts of Limited Liability Companies

41.1 A B The liability of a limited company (to pay debts) is not limited - it is the liability of shareholders in such a company which is limited (to any amount unpaid on their shares).

C The fact that the company is a legal entity separate and distinct from its owner(s) is considered to be an advantage of a limited company, relative to other forms of business organisation because it is this feature which allows shareholders' liability to be limited.

41.2 A B A person may be a director of a company and yet not own any shares in it.

C The term 'partner' is confined to partnerships. Two people may go into business together as business partners but if they set up a company and become shareholders and / or directors then the latter terms should be used when referring to them.

41.3 A Although the company can incur unlimited debts, which it is liable to pay, the shareholders will not become liable to pay them.

41.4 A Answer B (the amount called up on his / her shares) could equal the amount unpaid, but only if the shareholder has not paid any money.

41.5	B	Although shares in most PLCs are traded on a recognised Stock Exchange they do not have to be in order for the company to be a PLC.
41.6	C	Per the Companies Acts
41.7	B	This is the essence of a private company - the Companies Acts require that shares in a private company cannot be freely bought and sold by the public.
41.8	D	A company's authorised share capital can be increased, if the shareholders so approve, by vote.
41.9	D	The issued share capital of a company is the total amount of share capital, both ordinary share capital and preference share capital, which it has actually sold to shareholders.
	A	The amount of the issued share capital of a company may be less than, or equal to, the company's authorised share capital.
	B	The total issued share capital of a company cannot equal its issued preference share capital, because every company must have at least two ordinary shares.
	C	There is no relationship between the amount of the issued share capital of a company and its reserves.
41.10	A	Dividends are paid by companies to their shareholders (both owners of ordinary shares and owners of preference shares, where applicable) as a return on the investment they have made in the company.
	B	Interest paid by a company on its borrowings is an expense which is deducted when calculating profit whereas dividends are an appropriation of the profit earned by a company.
	C	Dividends may be paid by a company to banks and other creditors, but only if they are shareholders in the company.
41.11	B	Dividends are a share of profit not an expense. As the dividend is not yet paid but will be paid within one year it is a current liability.
	A	A dividend is an appropriation of profit, not an expense.
	C	The bank balance won't be reduced until the dividend is paid.
41.12	B	The declaration of a dividend means the announcement by the company of its intention to pay the dividend at some future date. Therefore, dividends are not paid for some time after they are declared. Consequently, at the time a dividend is declared it becomes an obligation to pay an amount of money at some future date i.e. a liability. It is also shown as an appropriation of profit.
	A	The company's bank balance will not be reduced until the dividend is actually paid.
	C	One of the effects of a company declaring a dividend is to reduce its retained profit (the second is the creation of a current liability). As the balance on the profit and loss account is part of the company's shareholders' funds, a reduction in this balance will reduce the company's shareholders' funds.
	D	As for answer C above.
41.13	B	The share capital account is credited with the nominal (par) value of the shares issued = 20,000 shares @ 25p each = £5,000. The premium on the issue will be credited to the share premium account (shown separately from share capital in the capital and reserves section of the balance sheet). The market value of share capital is not shown in the balance sheet.

41.14	C	The term 'shareholders' funds' means all of the money 'owed' by the company to its shareholders. This is the total of all money invested in the company by the shareholders (share capital) and all profits earned by the company (these profits are 'owned' by the company, which in turn is owned by its shareholders) which is the total of the balance on the profit and loss account (profits retained) and the balance on all other reserve accounts (amounts debited in the profit and loss appropriation account and transferred into the balance sheet).
41.15	D	The balance on the profit and loss account (part of shareholders' funds) will be reduced and the balance on the capital reserve account (also part of shareholders' funds) will be increased by the same amount.

41.16   C

Profit after tax	£26,600
Preference dividend (£20,000 * 8%)	- £1,600
	£25,000
Transfer to general reserve	- £5,000
Profit available to pay ordinary dividend	£20,000

As £20,000 is available for the payment of the dividend on the ordinary shares and the company wishes to pay the maximum possible dividend, £20,000 will be paid.

£20,000 dividend / £50,000 issued ordinary share capital = 40% ordinary dividend.

41.17   A

Preference dividend = £100,000 * 4% =	£4,000
Ordinary dividend = 100,000 shares * 10p each =	£10,000
(100,000 shares = £200,000 / £2 nominal (par) value)	£14,000

41.18   B   Earning a profit will increase revenue reserves while paying (or proposing) dividends will reduce revenue reserves. Therefore, revenue reserves at 31 December = revenue reserves at 1 January + profit - dividends.
Therefore, £31,000 = £15,000 + £27,000 - dividends.
Therefore, dividends = £11,000.

41.19   C

Preference dividend = £50,000 * 6% =	£3,000
Ordinary dividend = 200,000 shares * 10p =	£20,000
	£23,000

41.20   B
- A   The profit earned during the most recent accounting period is shown in the Profit and Loss Account.
- C   The balance on the profit and loss account is a profit or a loss - cash is not the same as profit.
- D   As for answer C above.

41.21   D   The company is being financed, in part, by the amount of its retained profit.
- A   Current liabilities are liabilities which are due to be discharged within one year.
- B   Fixed assets are assets which have an expected useful economic life of more than one year and were purchased in order to be used on a continuing basis rather than solely for resale.
- C   Current assets are cash and positive bank balances and other assets likely to be converted into cash or bank balances within a year as a result of normal trading operations.

41.22   C   Dividends payable are a current liability.

41.23   C   Remuneration paid to directors, during the current accounting period, in respect of the same period is an expense, and, just like any other expense, is charged as an expense in the profit and loss account (in accordance with the accruals concept).

41.24	D	Fixed assets are shown in the balance sheet at their net book value i.e. their cost or valuation less the cumulative provision for depreciation on them.
41.25	B	Debenture interest paid during the current accounting period, in respect of the same period is an expense, and, just like any other expense, is charged as an expense in the profit and loss account (in accordance with the accruals concept).
41.26	B	A Debenture interest paid during the current accounting period, in respect of the same period is an expense, and, just like any other expense, is charged as an expense in the profit and loss account (in accordance with the accruals concept) not the profit and loss appropriation account. C Remuneration paid to directors, during the current accounting period, in respect of the same period is an expense, and, just like any other expense, is charged as an expense in the profit and loss account (in accordance with the accruals concept) not the profit and loss appropriation account.
41.27	C	The market value of ordinary shares can change on a daily basis. Therefore, even if the market value at the end of the year was shown in the financial statements when they are being printed, this figure would be out of date by the time the financial statements were published. Therefore, while a market value could be shown in the financial statements, it cannot be the current market value. A The nominal (par) value of the issued ordinary share capital of the company is shown in the capital and reserves section of the balance sheet. B The (net) book value of the company's fixed assets is shown in the fixed assets section of the balance sheet.
41.28	D	The net assets of a company is the total of its assets less the total of its liabilities, that is, the total of the top part of the balance sheet. The (book value of the) shareholders' interest in the company (shareholders' funds) is the total of the (book value of the) capital contributed by them plus the company's reserves. This is also equal to the total of the capital and reserves section (bottom part) of the balance sheet. Since the top and bottom parts of the balance sheet must agree, the total of the net assets of a company must be equal to the book value of the shareholders' interest in the company.
41.29	A	In respect of any particular accounting period, dividends on preference shares, whether cumulative or non-cumulative, must be paid before any dividend can be paid on ordinary shares. If the company is unable to pay the dividend due on preference shares, whether cumulative or non-cumulative, it cannot pay a dividend on ordinary shares. In the case of non-cumulative preference shares, the shareholder's right to receive a dividend lapses. However, in the case of cumulative preference shares, the shareholder's right to receive a dividend does not lapse - and all such dividends must be paid before any dividend can be paid on ordinary shares in any future accounting period.
41.30	A	Money has been received - so the bank balance is increased. Shares have been issued - so the company's share capital has been increased.
41.31	C	Goodwill is the difference between the sum of the fair values of individual assets and liabilities and their purchase price. This difference can be either positive (in which case goodwill will be a debit balance) or negative (in which case goodwill will be a credit balance), depending on the purchase price.

41.32	A	B	If a company sells a fixed asset at a profit, the asset and the depreciation on it (if any) are removed from the balance sheet, the money received is added to the bank balance and the profit is shown in the profit and loss account. An asset disposal account is used to record the above.
		C	The market value of most companies' shares exceeds their nominal (par) value. However, as the market value is not shown in the financial statements this is of no significance from this point of view.
41.33	B		As goodwill will normally have an expected useful economic life of more than one year, it is a fixed asset. As it does not have physical substance, it is an intangible asset.
41.34	C	A	The Stock Exchange issues rules and regulations concerning the financial statements of PLCs whose shares are listed on the exchange.
		B	The government is responsible for preparing legislation.
41.35	C		No explanation required.
41.36	A		This is in accordance with the Explanatory Foreword to the accounting and financial reporting standards.
41.37	D	A	An Exposure Draft (ED) is what was issued prior to issuing a Statement of Standard Accounting Practice (SSAP). Such EDs are no longer issued as SSAPs are no longer issued.
		B	There is no such document in accounting.
		C	There is no such document in accounting.
41.38	B		The format of company financial statements throughout the EU was prescribed in the EC fourth directive on company law. This directive required all member states to issue national legislation containing the provisions of the directive. As a result, all member states now have legislation in place governing the format and content of the financial statements of companies.
41.39	A	B	Stock Exchange regulations apply only to companies whose shares are listed on the Exchange.
		C	Regulations issued by the Accounting Standards Board relate to the preparation of financial statements, not to their dissemination / publication.

Purchase of Existing Partnership and Sole Traders' Businesses

42.1	A	No explanation necessary.
42.2	B	No explanation necessary.

Cash Flow Statements: An Introduction

43.1   A   If fixed assets were purchased and paid for, the bank balance would disapprove. However, if they were not yet paid for, it would remain constant.

       B   An increase in a long-term bank loan means money has been received by the company. This money would normally be in a separate account, but even if it was lodged to the same account as the overdraft, it would improve the balance not disimprove it.

       C   A decrease in the company's debtors can arise only by debtors paying money to the company. This would improve the bank balance.

       D   An increase in the company's creditors will arise by making additional purchases without paying for them - which will not disimprove the bank balance.

43.2   C   A   The profitability or otherwise of a business' operations for a period of time is shown by its profit and loss account.

       B   The financial position of an entity at the end of an accounting period is shown by its balance sheet.

43.3   B   A   The Companies Acts require profit and loss accounts and balance sheets to be prepared but they do not require cash flow statements.

       C   Stock Exchange regulations apply to companies whose shares are listed on it. However, Cash Flow Statements are required for all entities, public and private, whose financial statements are intended to give a true and fair view of its profit or loss and financial position.

43.4   B   Some entities, the financial statements of which are beyond the scope of this book, for example, building societies and insurance companies, do not have to prepare cash flow statements.

43.5   C   A   The repayment of a bank loan is an outflow of cash.

       B   The charge for depreciation for the current year will be shown as part of the reconciliation of operating profit or loss to net cash flow from operating activities because, although it is an expense in the profit and loss account, unlike most other expenses, no money is paid out in respect of depreciation.

       D   The difference between the old and new valuations in the case of the revaluation of fixed assets is neither a cash inflow or outflow.

43.6   A   B   A decrease in trade debtors over the course of an accounting period will be shown as part of the reconciliation of operating profit or loss to net cash flow from operating activities.

       C   Money received as a result of issuing new shares is a cash inflow.

43.7   C   A   Not paying invoices received from creditors would not reduce the bank balance. In fact, the bank balance would be higher than if the invoices were paid.

       B   If money was received as a result of the sale of fixed assets during the period the bank balance would have improved. If they were sold on credit and payment has not yet been received the bank balance would be unaffected.

       D   An increase in the depreciation charge relative to the previous accounting period would not have any impact on the bank balance as depreciation is a 'non-cash' expense.

43.8	A	B An increase in trade debtors over the course of the period while sales remain constant means that money is being received less quickly than previously. This would lead to a disimprovement in the bank balance, given that outflows remain constant. If debtors had risen as a result of an even greater increase in sales, the bank balance could have improved - but it is the increase in sales, not the increase in debtors which would have caused it.
		C An increase in the value of stocks over the course of the period means that stock has been purchased. If this has been paid for, the bank balance will have disimproved. If it has not been paid for, there won't be any affect on the bank balance.
		D Paying trade creditors more quickly this period than in previous accounting periods means that money is leaving the business faster than before. This will lead to a disimprovement in the bank balance.
43.9	D	A Dividends paid are included under the heading 'Returns on Investments and Servicing of Finance'.
		B A new long-term loan taken out to finance the purchase of fixed assets is included under the heading 'Financing'.
		C Interest paid on a long-term bank loan is included under the heading 'Returns on Investments and Servicing of Finance'.
43.10	D	A Dividends paid are included under the heading 'Returns on Investments and Servicing of Finance'.
		B A new long-term loan taken out to finance the purchase of fixed assets is included under the heading 'Financing'.
		C Interest paid on a long-term bank loan is included under the heading 'Returns on Investments and Servicing of Finance'.
43.11	B	A Dividends paid are included under the heading 'Returns on Investments and Servicing of Finance'.
		C Interest paid on a long-term bank loan is included under the heading 'Returns on Investments and Servicing of Finance'.
		D The cost of purchasing a patent is included under the heading 'Investing Activities'.
43.12	B	One purpose of preparing a cash flow statement is to analyse the change (increase or decrease) in cash and cash equivalents. Therefore, the total of the five sub-headings must equal the increase or decrease in cash and cash equivalents.
43.13	C	Cash equivalents are short-term, highly liquid investments which are readily convertible into known amounts of cash without notice and which were within three months of maturity when acquired; less advances from banks repayable within three months from the date of the advance.
43.14	A	To see how a company, or its net investing activities, are being financed, one needs to look at all of the principal sources of cash. These are operating activities and financing activities.
43.15	B	A loan is a source of finance and all cash inflows and outflows associated with financing should be shown in the financing section of the cash flow statement.
43.16	D	As a scrip issue of shares does not result in any cash inflow or outflow it should not be shown in a cash flow statement.

43.17	B	Working capital, being the difference between the total of current assets and that of current liabilities, consists of stock, debtors, bank, cash, creditors etc. The changes in the non-cash and cash equivalent items are shown as part of the reconciliation of the operating profit or loss to the net cash flow from operating activities. Any change in the cash and cash equivalent items equals the final total of the cash flow statement. This final total is analysed in the notes to the cash flow statement.
43.18	A	All money received, irrespective of its source, should be shown as a cash inflow.
43.19	A	All profits and losses on the sale of fixed assets are included in the reconciliation of operating profit or loss to net cash flow from operating activities.
	B	Any change in a provision for doubtful debts is included in the reconciliation of the operating profit or loss to the net cash flow from operating activities but the provision itself is not.
	C	An increase in the valuation of fixed assets arising from a revaluation does not give rise to a cash inflow, cash outflow, or effect on profit. It should not therefore be included in the cash flow statement.
	D	It is the change in the value of stock from the beginning of the period covered by the cash flow statement to the end of that period which is included in the reconciliation of the operating profit or loss to the net cash flow from operating activities. Therefore, an adjustment made to write-down the valuation of stocks to net realisable value, will be included in this reconciliation if it is the sole reason for the change in the value of stock over the course of the accounting period.
43.20	C	An increase in a company's authorised share capital does not give rise to any cash inflow or outflow. Only when the shares are issued will a cash (inflow) arise.
	A	An increase in the share premium account can arise only as a result of issuing shares at a premium. The money received in respect of these shares is a cash inflow.
	B	Upon the issue of debentures, money is received from the financial institution(s) which issued them - this is a cash inflow.
	D	Proceeds arising from the issue of new preference shares is clearly a cash inflow.

An Introduction to the Analysis and Interpretation of Accounting Statements

44.1	C	Liquidity means the capacity of an entity to pay its debts as they become due. As the current ratio compares an entity's current assets with its current liabilities it shows whether those current assets are sufficient to meet short-term (current) liabilities i.e. it is a measure of short-term liquidity.
44.2	D	A (Current assets : Current liabilities) is the current ratio.
		B (Debtors : Creditors) is not any commonly recognised accounting ratio.
		C (Current assets less debtors : Current liabilities) is not any commonly recognised accounting ratio.
44.3	C	Acid-test ratio = (Current Assets - Stock) : Current Liabilities
		A Stock is clearly excluded from the calculation.
		B Debentures are a long-term liability.
44.4	A	Acid-test Ratio = (Current Assets - Stock) : Current Liabilities = (£60,000 - £10,000) : £20,000 = 2.5 : 1

44.5	C	'Return' means the net profit earned, without adjustment. Capital employed means the average capital.
44.6	B	The average number of days which an entity takes to pay its creditors during an accounting period is given by its creditors to purchases ratio.
44.7	A	The average debtors' collection period during an accounting period is given by the debtors to sales ratio.
44.8	B	Stock turnover = Cost of sales / Average stock Cost of sales = Stock at the beginning of the period + Purchases during the period - Stock at the end of the period Average stock = (Stock at the beginning of the period + Stock at the end of the period) / 2 Stock turnover = (£25,000 + £200,000 - £35,000) / £30,000 = 6.33 times
44.9	A	Gearing Ratio = Loan capital : Total capital = 3 : 5 Therefore, loan capital = 3 / (3+5) = 3 / 8 = 37.5%
44.10	C	Even though the abbreviation stands for Earnings Per Share, it generally means earnings per ordinary share.
44.11	A	EPS = Profit attributable to ordinary shareholders / No. of ordinary shares issued.
44.12	B	EPS = Profit attributable to ordinary shareholders / No. of ordinary shares issued Debenture interest has already been deducted in arriving at net profit. Attributable profit = Net profit after tax - Preference dividends = £480,000 - £4,800 = £475,200 EPS = £475,200 / 200,000 ordinary shares = £2.376
44.13	B	Acid-test ratio = (Current Assets - Stock) : Current Liabilities = (£50,000 - £10,000) : £25,000 = 1.6 : 1. The data given for rate of stock turnover, average stock and sales are all irrelevant.
44.14	C	Stock turnover = Cost of sales / Average stock Average stock = £10,000 Stock Turnover during the year = 7 times Therefore, cost of sales = £70,000. Normally, Cost of sales = Opening stock + Purchases - Closing stock. As this is the first year of business, there is no opening stock. Closing stock = £10,000. Therefore, £70,000 = purchases - £10,000 Therefore, purchases = £80,000
44.15	C	Period of credit given = (Debtors / Credit sales) * 365 = (£5,000 / £84,000) * 365 = 22 days approx.
44.16	D	Average rate of stock turnover = Cost of sales / Average Stock. Cost of sales = Sales - Gross profit = £700,000. Average stock = (opening stock + closing stock) / 2 = (£190,000 + £210,000) / 2 = £200,000. Average rate of stock turnover = £700,000 / £200,000 = 3.50 times
44.17	A	Average collection period = (Average Debtors / Credit sales) * 365 Average Debtors = [(£172,500 + £218,500) / 2] * 100 / 115) = £170,000. Credit sales = £1,000,000 * 85% = £850,000. Average collection period = £170,000 / £850,000 * 365 = 73 days

| 44.18 | A | Average payment period = (Average Creditors / Credit purchases) * 365
Average Creditors = [(£230,000 + £184,000) / 2] * 100 / 115) = £180,000.
Cost of sales = Sales - Gross profit = £700,000.
Cost of sales = opening stock + purchases - closing stock.
£700,000 = £165,000 + purchases - £185,000.
Therefore, purchases = £720,000.
Average payment period = £180,000 / £720,000 * 365 = 91 days |
|---|---|---|
| 44.19 | B | Dividend yield = Dividend per share / Market price per share.
Dividend per share = EPS / Dividend cover = 32p / 2 = 16p
Dividend Yield = 16p / £4.00 = 4% |
| 44.20 | C | Because Interest Cover is intended to indicate the ability of a firm to pay its interest bill, the profit figure used in its calculation must be the profit out of which interest is to be paid, that is, its profit before paying tax and before paying interest. The interest expense is added to the net profit figure because 'net profit' means profit after deducting all expenses, including interest. |
| 44.21 | D | Industry average measures are most useful because they focus specifically on the industry being analysed.

A Rule-of-thumb measures such as 'the current ratio should be 2 : 1' are not particularly useful in this case since they do not relate specifically to the industry being analysed. Furthermore, the performance of any given industry will change over time.

B Measures of the past performance of the business will give an indication of whether the business is improving or disimproving over time but are of no use when comparing a specific business to its competitors.

C As for answer B above, measures which are confined to a single business are of no use when comparing that business to its competitors. |
| 44.22 | B | If the business uses accounting methods which are not acceptable, for example, does not depreciate its buildings, its profit and loss account (and balance sheet) will not be correct.

A So long as acceptable accounting methods are used, the countries in which the business operates will not affect the *accuracy* of its profit figure.

C So long as acceptable accounting methods are used, the industry in which the business operates will not affect the *accuracy* of its profit figure. |
| 44.23 | C | Working capital is the amount by which total current assets exceeds total current liabilities. Therefore, an increase in working capital requires an increase in current assets relative to any change in current liabilities.

A the purchase of fixed assets on credit during the period, if paid for, would reduce the bank balance, thus reducing working capital. If not paid for, it would increase creditors, also reducing working capital.

B the purchase of fixed assets by cheque during the period, would reduce the bank balance, thus reducing working capital. |
| 44.24 | B | The current ratio is calculated as (Current Assets : Current Liabilities). A payment to a creditor of £1,000 will reduce the cash or bank balance (current assets) and reduce creditors (a current liability) by this amount. If, before the payment, the total of current liabilities exceeds that of current assets then the relative effect on current assets is greater than it is on current liabilities, thus reducing the current ratio. For example, if, before the payment, current liabilities totalled £10,000 and current assets totalled £8,000 (giving a current ratio of 0.8 : 1), then, after the payment, the current ratio would be £7,000 : £9,000 = .777 : 1. |

44.25 A   The current ratio is calculated as (Current Assets : Current Liabilities). Payment of a dividend, which has already been proposed, will reduce the bank balance (a current asset) and reduce proposed dividends (a current liability) by the same amount, thus having no effect on the current ratio. For example, if, before the payment, current assets totalled £150,000 and current liabilities totalled £100,000 the situation would be as follows:

	Current Assets	Current Liabilities	Current Ratio
Before the payment	£150,000	£100,000	1.5 : 1
After the payment	£100,000	£50,000	2 : 1

44.26 A   The current ratio is calculated as (Current Assets : Current Liabilities) and the acid-test ratio is calculated as [(Current Assets - Stock) : Current Liabilities]. Payment of a dividend, which has already been proposed, will reduce the bank balance (a current asset) and reduce proposed dividends (a current liability) by the same amount, thus having no effect on the current ratio. As payment of the dividend has no effect on stock, the acid-test ratio will also remain the same. For example, if, before the payment, current assets totalled £150,000 and current liabilities totalled £100,000 the situation would be as follows:

	Current Assets - Stock*	Current Liabilities	Acid-test Ratio
Before the payment	£70,000	£100,000	0.7 : 1
After the payment	£20,000	£50,000	0.4 : 1

* Stock has to be £80,000 if the current ratio is 1.5 : 1 and the acid-test ratio is 0.7 : 1

44.27 A   The current ratio is calculated as (Current Assets : Current Liabilities). The effect of purchasing stock and paying for it, is to increase stock and reduce bank by the same amount. This does not have any effect on current liabilities and the two effects on current assets - the increase in stock and the decrease in the bank balance - cancel each other out - leaving the total of current assets unchanged.

44.28 A   The acid-test ratio is calculated as (Current Assets - Stock) : Current Liabilities. The effect of purchasing stock and paying for it is to increase stock by £2,000 and to reduce the bank balance by the same amount. Although this does not have any effect on the current ratio (as the total of both current assets and current liabilities remains constant) it does have an effect on the acid-test ratio as the total of 'current assets - stock' declines. For example, if, before this transaction took place the business' current assets consisted of its £4,000 bank balance and stock of £2,000 and its current liabilities totalled £4,000 then its acid-test ratio would be as follows:

	Current Assets - Stock	Current Liabilities	Acid-test Ratio
Before the purchase	£4,000	£4,000	1 : 1
After the purchase	£2,000	£4,000	0.5 : 1

44.29 C   The current ratio is calculated as (Current Assets : Current Liabilities) and the acid-test ratio is calculated as [(Current Assets - Stock) : Current Liabilities]. Payment of a dividend will reduce the bank balance and reduce proposed dividends by the same absolute amount. If, before the payment, the total of current liabilities exceeds that of current assets then the relative effect on current assets is greater than it is on current liabilities. In exams, it is easiest to figure out this type of question by putting numbers on it.

44.30 C   The current ratio is calculated as (Current Assets : Current Liabilities). Payment of a dividend will reduce the bank balance and reduce proposed dividends by the same absolute amount. If, before the payment, the total of current liabilities exceeds that of current assets then the relative effect on current assets is greater than it is on current liabilities. In exams, it is easiest to figure out this type of question by putting numbers on it.

Accounting Theory

45.1	B	No explanation necessary.
45.2	B	No explanation necessary.
45.3	B	A this is historical cost (or a revalued amount) less accumulated depreciation (if any).
		C this is the replacement cost of the item.

Answers - Quick Reference Table

Explanations of answers are given on pages 101-154.

Q	A	Q	A	Q	A	Q	A	Q	A	Q	A	Q	A	Q	A
1.1	A	8.11	D	16.1	C	23.13	C	28.7	C	33.2	B	40.1	B	43.9	D
1.2	D	8.12	D	16.2	D	23.14	A	28.8	B	33.3	A	40.2	C	43.10	D
1.3	D	8.13	C	16.3	B	23.15	B	28.9	A	33.4	C	41.1	A	43.11	B
1.4	A	8.14	D	16.4	A	23.16	C	28.10	B	33.5	D	41.2	A	43.12	B
1.5	B	9.1	A	16.5	A	24.1	A	28.11	B	33.6	B	41.3	A	43.13	C
1.6	A	9.2	C	17.1	C	24.2	B	28.12	B	33.7	A	41.4	A	43.14	A
1.7	B	9.3	A	17.2	B	24.3	B	28.13	B	33.8	D	41.5	B	43.15	B
1.8	C	9.4	D	18.1	B	24.4	C	28.14	A	34.1	A	41.6	C	43.16	D
1.9	D	9.5	B	18.2	B	24.5	B	29.1	C	34.2	A	41.7	B	43.17	B
2.1	A	9.6	D	19.1	C	24.6	B	29.2	D	34.3	B	41.8	D	43.18	A
2.2	B	9.7	B	19.2	B	24.7	B	29.3	B	34.4	B	41.9	D	43.19	A
2.3	A	9.8	C	19.3	C	24.8	C	29.4	D	34.5	A	41.10	A	43.20	C
2.4	B	9.9	B	19.4	B	24.9	A	29.5	C	34.6	D	41.11	B	44.1	C
2.5	C	9.10	A	19.5	A	24.10	C	29.6	A	35.1	B	41.12	B	44.2	D
2.6	D	10.1	C	19.6	B	24.11	D	29.7	D	35.2	B	41.13	B	44.3	C
3.1	C	10.2	C	19.7	D	24.12	B	29.8	C	35.3	B	41.14	C	44.4	A
3.2	D	10.3	C	19.8	B	25.1	C	29.9	D	35.4	A	41.15	D	44.5	C
3.3	A	10.4	C	19.9	B	25.2	C	29.10	A	35.5	A	41.16	C	44.6	B
3.4	B	10.5	C	19.10	B	25.3	D	29.11	C	35.6	B	41.17	A	44.7	A
3.5	B	10.6	A	19.11	C	25.4	C	30.1	B	35.7	A	41.18	B	44.8	B
3.6	C	10.7	B	19.12	A	25.5	C	30.2	C	35.8	C	41.19	C	44.9	A
3.7	D	10.8	A	19.13	A	25.6	C	30.3	D	35.9	B	41.20	B	44.10	C
4.1	D	10.9	C	19.14	B	25.7	D	30.4	C	36.1	A	41.21	D	44.11	A
4.2	C	10.10	C	19.15	B	26.1	C	30.5	C	36.2	A	41.22	C	44.12	B
4.3	B	10.11	A	19.16	B	26.2	C	30.6	D	36.3	C	41.23	C	44.13	B
4.4	C	11.1	B	19.17	C	26.3	C	30.7	B	36.4	C	41.24	D	44.14	C
5.1	B	11.2	C	19.18	C	26.4	B	30.8	C	36.5	D	41.25	B	44.15	C
5.2	A	11.3	C	19.19	D	26.5	D	30.9	C	36.6	A	41.26	B	44.16	D
5.3	C	11.4	A	19.20	A	27.1	D	30.10	B	36.7	B	41.27	C	44.17	A
5.4	A	11.5	C	19.21	C	27.2	D	30.11	C	36.8	B	41.28	C	44.18	A
6.1	D	12.1	A	20.1	B	27.3	A	30.12	D	36.9	A	41.29	A	44.19	B
6.2	A	12.2	A	21.1	A	27.4	A	30.13	B	36.10	A	41.30	A	44.20	C
6.3	C	12.3	C	21.2	B	27.5	D	30.14	C	36.11	D	41.31	C	44.21	D
6.4	B	12.4	C	21.3	C	27.6	C	30.15	B	36.12	D	41.32	A	44.22	B
6.5	C	12.5	C	21.4	A	27.7	B	30.16	B	36.13	C	41.33	B	44.23	C
6.6	A	12.6	B	21.5	C	27.8	C	30.17	B	36.14	B	41.34	C	44.24	B
6.7	C	12.7	C	22.1	B	27.9	A	30.18	C	36.15	C	41.35	C	44.25	A
7.1	B	12.8	B	22.2	B	27.10	B	30.19	C	36.16	D	41.36	A	44.26	A
7.2	D	12.9	C	22.3	A	27.11	B	30.20	A	37.1	A	41.37	D	44.27	A
7.3	C	13.1	B	23.1	B	27.12	A	30.21	A	37.2	B	41.38	B	44.28	A
7.4	A	13.2	C	23.2	A	27.13	B	30.22	A	38.1	C	41.39	A	44.29	C
8.1	C	13.3	A	23.3	A	27.14	C	30.23	C	38.2	A	42.1	A	44.30	C
8.2	C	13.4	A	23.4	A	27.15	B	31.1	D	38.3	A	42.2	B	45.1	B
8.3	C	13.5	C	23.5	D	27.16	A	31.2	C	38.4	D	43.1	A	45.2	B
8.4	B	13.6	A	23.6	C	27.17	A	31.3	C	38.5	C	43.2	C	45.3	B
8.5	B	14.1	B	23.7	B	28.1	D	32.1	D	38.6	D	43.3	B		
8.6	C	14.2	C	23.8	C	28.2	A	32.2	A	38.7	B	43.4	B		
8.7	B	14.3	A	23.9	B	28.3	C	32.3	B	38.8	B	43.5	C		
8.8	D	15.1	A	23.10	B	28.4	A	32.4	D	39.1	C	43.6	A		
8.9	A	15.2	D	23.11	D	28.5	C	32.5	C	39.2	A	43.7	C		
8.10	B	15.3	C	23.12	B	28.6	C	33.1	A	39.3	A	43.8	A		